Perspectives on school effectiveness
and school improvement

Perspectives on school effectiveness and school improvement

Michael Barber (editor)
John White (editor)
Louise Stoll
Peter Mortimore
Lynn Davies
Christopher Winch
Pam Sammons
Josh Hillman
David Hamilton
Michael Fielding
David Scott

INSTITUTE OF
EDUCATION
UNIVERSITY OF LONDON

Bedford Way Papers

First published in 1997 by the Institute of Education University of London,
20 Bedford Way, London WC1H 0AL

Pursuing Excellence in Education

© Institute of Education University of London 1997

British Library Cataloguing in Publication Data;
a catalogue record for this publication is available from the British Library

ISBN 85473 501 1

Design and Typography by Joan Rose

Produced by Reprographic Services
Institute of Education
20 Bedford Way
LondonWC1H 0AL

Printed by Formara Limited
16 The Candlemakers, Temple Farm Industrial Estate
Southend on Sea, Essex SS2 5RX

June 1997

Contents

Acknowledgements

The editors are grateful to the following organizations and journals for permission to republish several of the papers in this book. To the Institute of Education, University of London for Louise Stoll and Peter Mortimore 'School effectiveness and school improvement'; to *Forum* for David Hamilton 'Peddling feel-good fictions' (Vol 38. No.2 1996); and for Pamela Sammons, Peter Mortimore and Josh Hillman 'Key characteristics of effective schools: a response to *Peddling feel-good fictions*' (Vol 38. No.3 1996); to OFSTED and the Institute of Education, University of London for Pamela Sammons, Peter Mortimore and Josh Hillman *Key characteristics of effective schools.* A slightly different version of Lynn Davies 'The rise of the school effectiveness movement' appeared in her book *Beyond Authoritarian School Management* (Ticknall: Education Now Books, 1994).

About the contributors

Michael Barber is Head of the Standards and Effectiveness Unit at the Department for Education and Employment, and Professor of Education at the Institute of Education, University of London.

Lynn Davies is Professor of International Education at the School of Education, University of Birmingham.

Michael Fielding is Lecturer in Education at the University of Cambridge Institute of Education.

David Hamilton is Professor of Education at the University of Liverpool.

Josh Hillman is Research Fellow/Officer at the Institute for Public Policy Research, London.

Peter Mortimore is Director of the Institute of Education, University of London.

Pam Sammons is Associate Director of the International School Effectiveness and Improvement Centre, Institute of Education, University of London.

David Scott is Lecturer in Education at the Institute of Education, University of London.

Louise Stoll is Lecturer in Education at the Institute of Education, University of London.

John White is Professor of Philosophy of Education at the Institute of Education, University of London.

Christopher Winch is Professor of Philosophy of Education at Nene College, Northampton.

Introduction

Michael Barber
John White

Research on school effectiveness and school improvement has become a major industry, not only in the United Kingdom but also in Australia, Canada, the United States and Holland. Although it took a decade or more to happen, that body of research has now had a major impact on policy at national, local and school level. The Department for Education and Employment established a School Effectiveness Division in 1994 which has become increasingly influential in the years since then. It has sought explicitly to learn from the research on school effectiveness and school improvement and to apply its lessons to policy on, for example, failing schools. The School Curriculum and Assessment Authority, meanwhile, has encouraged further research into value-added indicators.

The revival of local education authorities in recent years has been built around the same body of research. Indeed, it would only be a slight exaggeration to say that it saved them from extinction. Meanwhile, in schools the level of interest in school effectiveness and improvement is higher than ever, not least because of the combination of delegated budgets and heightened pressures for accountability.

It is hard to think of another example of a body of research having such a powerful impact on the education service since the war. Such pre-eminence brings with it inevitable risks. Qualified findings of one research study may become perceived as accepted truths. The often controversial assumptions behind a body of work may go undebated. In addition, policy-makers and journalists may start simplifying research and quoting it out of context.

All of these have occurred in this country in recent years. This does not mean that those who undertake work in this field should stop doing so or that they should stop promoting the findings of their research. It does mean that, as they do so, they need to remain conscious of the limits as well as the potential of their research and to be aware of critiques that have been made of their methods, assumptions and findings. The Institute of Education is a global leader in the field of school effectiveness and school improvement. The contributions of Peter Mortimore, Harvey Goldstein, Pam Sammons, Sally Thomas, Louise Stoll and Kate Myers, for example, are internationally respected. The Institute is also much more than this. It has an unrivalled breadth and depth of scholarship in sociology, history, psychology and philosophy of education among other areas of study. It is, therefore, the ideal centre in which to produce a book such as this one. Its purpose is to promote dialogue between school effectiveness and school improvement researchers and their critics. It has been produced in the best spirit of proper academic debate and will, we hope, lead to a refined discourse about school effectiveness and school improvement and to further reflection and discussion about a developing body of research which is likely to maintain a high profile well into the next century.

Critical voices

The 'perspectives' of this book's title are those of contributors to research in school effectiveness and school improvement (SESI) as well as those of their recent critics. The following ten chapters embrace:

- summaries of the research (Chapters 1 and 5)
- critical commentaries on it (Chapters 2, 3, 4, 6, 8 and 9)
- replies to these (Chapters 7 and 10).

The first chapter, 'School effectiveness and school improvement', sets the scene with a broad, non-technical survey of work in both these areas. It was originally published by the Institute of Education in 1995 as the second in its *Viewpoint* series, designed to bring up-to-date research in different areas of educational study to a wider public. In this chapter, Louise Stoll and Peter Mortimore begin with definitions of the two areas and outline their aims. Here they present an account of the role of value-added analyses in school effectiveness research (SER) and a brief historical sketch of research on school improvement (SI). They go on to discuss the 'doors' to SI, openable by those inside the school as well as by agencies, like the inspectorate, outside it. Their table of factors identified by research as conducive to SESI will be useful to readers of some of the later essays in this book, as much of the criticism and response to criticism revolves around these. The second part of the essay looks at current research and development, including attempts to bring the two paradigms closer together, as well as providing a detailed compilation of research projects, networks, courses and resources across Britain. A final section is about future needs and focuses on ways of speeding up school improvement, the need to investigate classrooms as well as the whole school, inside versus outside measures to improve schools, and the need for an adequate underpinning theory.

Lynn Davies's essay is an updated and revised version of a chapter she wrote in *Beyond Authoritarian School Management*. (Davies 1994). That book is on school management and the present essay looks at SER from the management point of view. The link between the two concerns is clear: if SER can identify the levers which need to be operated in order to make a school more effective, not least those with fewer resource implications, this information can be very useful to those responsible for running schools. The chapter begins with a lucid summary of how the research works, paying particular attention to the factors in effective schooling and the difficulty of coming up with a list of them that applies across the globe. Here, as throughout the essay, evidence is drawn from research in many different countries, not least in developing countries.

The essay goes on to look at various kinds of problems with SER. It points to the narrowness of using measurable outcomes and to the broader educational goals favoured by different countries. Technical problems include the difficulty of treating factors as isolable phenomena, as well as the gap between a factor's being associated with a certain outcome and its being causally productive of it. There are also problems about how SER is translated into school improvement schemes. The author cautions against crude attempts to operate the factor-levers and calls for flexibility and sensitivity to the particularities of a school culture. The last problem that she raises is the lack of a political analysis: the research is concerned with 'what works', not 'with the question of in whose interests it works'. She concludes that SER should neither be abandoned nor made statistically more sophisticated: it should be geared to goals that communities actually want – goals that stress personal qualities as well as intellectual achievements – and should ideally be carried out by school communities themselves.

The wider context of John White's chapter is the illumination he claims philosophy of education can shed on educational research. The specific focus is the conceptualization of recent work in SE and SI. Is 'effectiveness' a value-neutral term, having to do only with causal relationships between means and ends? Or does it carry connotations of desirability? Are all the factors revealed by SER which make for an effective school the kinds of phenomena which require empirical investigation to discover them? Or can some of them be found out by a priori reflection (which White explicitly distinguishes from common sense)? Why does SER limit itself to short-term outcomes, like pupils' performance in public examinations? Could it throw light on the success of schools in attaining longer-term educational goals, such as the promotion of democratic citizenship?

The second part of the essay turns initially to SI. It suggests that this needs to be conceived more broadly than within a SE framework, outlining a thought-structure in which it should operate, which begins with fundamental considerations about the aims of education and ends with practical considerations about the procedures by which these aims and the sub-aims they generate could be realized. The last section of the chapter raises methodological issues about SESI research. It advocates more attention to practical reasoning in the Aristotelian tradition at the expense of currently favoured science-based approaches and is sceptical whether SESI research is, as has been claimed, in need of an overarching theory.

Christopher Winch's contribution in Chapter 4 relates SER to issues of accountability. It is concerned, first, with what he terms 'constitutive' accountability through its assessments of the rate of progress in academic achievement that pupils make in their schools. Winch's outline of the difficulties in conducting 'value-added' research leads him to call for OFSTED to be as methodologically cautious in its judgements of schools as SER researchers have been. This leads him into a broader discussion of whether SER results should be disseminated to the public. He concludes that both one-shot results and an elementary form of value-added data are important instruments of constitutive accountability.

SESI research is also concerned with 'qualitative' accountability, that is with how school provision can be improved. Winch, like Davies and White, discusses the factors promoting effective schools. He points out that, while some would see factors like orderly classrooms or a stress on academic achievement as merely reflecting common sense, others on the more child-centred wing might brand these as authoritarian. This leads to his suggestion that, behind its esoteric scientific data, SER may be in the business of introducing or reinforcing contested, and politically sensitive, views about how schools should be run. Winch urges SE researchers to become more explicit about their educational aims: if a theory of school effectiveness is now needed (see also White), it should be about such underlying aims and values. SER 'cannot continue developing esoteric technical expertise and ignoring wider political and philosophical issues about the nature and future direction of the education service'.

Chapters 5, 6 and 7 belong together. Chapter 6 is a critique of a review of SER republished here in Chapter 5, and Chapter 7 is a reply to the critique by the authors of the review.

The SER review, by Pam Sammons, Josh Hillman and Peter Mortimore, was carried out by the Institute of Education for OFSTED and published in April 1995 under the title *Key Characteristics of Effective Schools*. The aim of the review was to provide 'an analysis of the key determinants of school effectiveness in secondary and primary schools'. It gives a fuller and more fully referenced survey of many of the themes picked out more briefly in Chapter 1. While there are useful discussions of the historical background of SER research, of its aims and definitions and methodology, the bulk of the essay is devoted to 11 'factors for effective schools'. These are almost identical to the factors outlined in Chapter 1 and mentioned earlier. The treatment of them is, however, much more detailed than in that chapter and, at every point, the specifics are tied firmly into the available research data. Interestingly for this present collection the authors' conclusion attempts among other matters to deal with criticisms that research findings about factors in SE are just a matter of common sense.

David Hamilton's critique of *Key Characteristics of Effective Schools* constitutes Chapter 6. Originally published in *Forum* in summer 1996, it is a brief, but forcefully worded, wholescale dismissal of SER. Hamilton regards it as 'an ethnocentric pseudo-science that serves merely to mystify anxious administrators and marginalize classroom practitioners'. Like many of the other critics in these pages, he has particular difficulties with the treatment of the 'key factors', in his case claiming to discern in it a 'sleight of hand' that fudges the distinction between correlates and determinants.

The three authors of *Key Characteristics of Effective Schools* produce a measured reply to Hamilton's charges in Chapter 7. Their response appeared first in the subsequent issue of *Forum* in autumn 1996. As well as putting forward more specific counterarguments, more generally they firmly reject the charge of ethnocentricity and underline the commitment to equity and democracy which powers the research.

Michael Fielding's essay is entitled 'Beyond school effectiveness and school improvement: lighting the slow fuse of possibility'. Its core is a discussion of a particular approach to school improvement he and other colleagues have been recently conducting at Cambridge University called IQEA (Improving the Quality of Education for All) and an account of a 'transformative education' which would go beyond this. He is critical of SER for reasons, partly connected with ones raised also by Davies and by Winch, to do with its absorption in sophisticated mathematical analysis at the expense of larger political concerns and with its insensitivity to the nuances and particularities of everyday school life.

He describes in some detail the mapping techniques developed at Cambridge, designed to encourage school staffs to reflect on the culture and structures of their schools and on changes within them, and argues that they constitute a more teacher-friendly approach to school improvement. Among other virtues, they preserve the thick texture of school life and help to reveal multiple perspectives and different assumptions. Fielding's 'transformative' proposals add student involvement to teacher involvement. They call for dialogue with students to be not an occasional feature of some lessons but an institutional requirement, connected with a view of education as a key element in the development of a democratic society. They differ from SE-based views on school improvement by being concerned not just with schooling but with the broader category of education, by resting on explicit values and by reflecting emancipatory educational commitments.

Chapter 9, by David Scott, is about methodological issues, drawing attention to what he calls 'the missing hermeneutical dimension in mathematical modelling of school effectiveness'. SER takes as its index of pupils' achievements their performance on various tasks. This can be quantified more easily than their competence in the area. Performance is not always a good guide to competence, yet when we are interested in what pupils learn, it is improvements in their abilities or competences which most concern us. SER also neglects curriculum factors among the factors promoting effective schools. It works with a behavioural objectives model of curriculum design and a technical rationalist view of pedagogy, both of which are open to basic objections.

Scott also explores the issue raised by Davies, about the relationship between correlations and causal mechanisms, drawing on Bhaskar's notion of the 'ontic fallacy'. While science deals in closed systems in which observed regularities and underlying causal mechanisms coincide, social research, as Giddens argues, is essentially hermeneutical. It depends on researchers understanding the perceptions, beliefs and intentions of the subjects being investigated (e.g. teachers in a school), as well as the researchers' own reflection on, and monitoring of, their own actions. This cannot be captured by mathematical modelling appropriate to a closed system. (There is a clear connection here with what Fielding has to say about the IQEA research, as well as with points raised by Davies about the particularities of school cultures.)

Peter Mortimore and Pam Sammons were invited to respond to their critics in this collection in an 'Endpiece' (Chapter 10). As they point out, SER has had its fair (or perhaps not so fair?) share of critics, ranging from university academics to Chris Woodhead of OFSTED and Melanie Phillips in the Observer. The authors discuss the main issues that the papers in this book have raised – about how effectiveness is to be defined, the methodology of the research, the charge that SER focuses on too narrow a range of outcomes, the neglect of process, whether empirical research is necessary to identify the factors associated with effectiveness, and whether SER is insufficiently concerned with equity. They reject the accusation that SE researchers have been uncritically supportive of recent government policy and conclude with wider observations about the responsibilities of academics on politically sensitive issues.

No doubt the critics of SER in this collection would welcome the chance to reply to these counterarguments. But this will have to be elsewhere: an 'Endpiece' is an 'Endpiece'. At least we hope that the often stark confrontations of argument and evidence that run through these pages will both clarify what is at stake and stimulate yet further debate.

Michael Barber
John White
1997

1 School effectiveness and school improvement

Louise Stoll
Peter Mortimore

Introduction

The last decade has seen a burgeoning of interest in the twin fields of school effectiveness and school improvement by politicians, policy-makers and practitioners. For some, the drive has been to raise standards and increase accountability through inspection and assessment measures, believing that the incentive of accountability and market competition will lead to improvement. Alternatively, reform and restructuring have led many people in schools to create their own agenda and to ask, 'How do we know that what we are doing makes a positive difference to our pupils?' and 'What can we do to provide pupils with the best possible education?'

This paper explores the two paradigms that underpin notions of school effectiveness and school improvement. We start with their definitions and aims. Key factors of effectiveness and improvement are examined and fundamental issues discussed. We conclude with a description of attempts to link the two areas of work.

School effectiveness: definition and aims

A basic definition of 'effectiveness' is 'the production of a desired result or outcome' (Levine and Lezotte, 1990). School effectiveness researchers aim to ascertain whether differential resources, processes and organizational arrangements affect student outcomes and, if so, how. Ultimately, school effectiveness research searches for appropriate and reliable ways to measure school quality. The concept of 'effectiveness' forces choices to be made among competing values. While some people choose a narrow approach with a basic-skills emphasis, others perceive schools' aims to be more diverse. There is a difference between those who believe that the chief focus of effectiveness should be equity, in particular, raising standards for students 'at risk', and those who are committed to increasing standards for all children. Both approaches are important and can, to a certain extent, be combined. In this paper we define an effective school as one in which pupils progress further than might be expected from consideration of its intake.

Research on school effectiveness

School effectiveness studies largely came about in reaction to the view that home background had a far greater influence on a child's development than did the school. This led to studies seeking to distinguish the impact of family background from that of the school, to ascertain whether some schools were more effective than others and, if so, to identify which factors contributed to the positive effects. Earlier studies, criticized for lack of generalizability and for methodological inadequacies, gave way to more sophisticated designs. Currently, school effectiveness researchers devote much attention to issues of measurement of student outcomes, stability and continuity of school effects, differential effectiveness and context specificity.

Value-added analyses

Value added is a technique designed to make fair comparisons between schools. It yields estimates of average progress for each institution. To assess the 'value' added by the school, it is essential to adjust for various background factors and for prior attainment by the individual child. To assess effectiveness of different schools without taking such information into account is like comparing apples with oranges. Unless schools are compared on a 'like with like' basis, judgements are neither fair nor valid. Increasingly in Britain, schools, local education authorities, the media and, recently, the government have been looking for ways to establish measures to use in the analysis of educational outcomes (DFE, 1995). These measures range from simple disaggregation of academic results and attendance in formation by, for example, sex, year and ethnic background, to the use of sophisticated multilevel modelling techniques.

Increasing consensus from political parties on the need for account to be taken of context in analysis of schools' performance is welcome. While this is a step in the right direction, unresolved issues remain around the use of the concept of value added.

- There is little agreement as to what academic measures are suitable for baseline assessment of pupils at the start of infant and junior school. Many tests are seen as inappropriate for young children.

- Current league tables and many of the available value-added analyses focus on examination and test results and attendance. While pupil attitudes are increasingly seen as an important aspect of a school's performance, less work has been done by researchers in terms of a corresponding value-added analysis. Furthermore, the world beyond school increasingly seeks young people who can display a wide range of skills and aptitudes, including the ability to solve problems, be flexible, creative and cooperative. These have been given scant attention in terms of the measures generally used in schools.

- Even when value-added analyses are used to produce 'adjusted' league tables, results need to be interpreted cautiously because confidence intervals for school 'effects' are wide. This means that many schools cannot be separated reliably and that only extreme schools or departments can be identified as performing much better or worse than predicted (Goldstein and Thomas, 1995).

Stability and continuity in schools' effectiveness

Despite variations in estimates of the stability of school effects over time, there is general agreement that it is important to take account of students' performance over a period of years, when judging a school's effectiveness.

evidence also suggests a lingering effect of primary school ᴛ ᴏhout a pupil's career in secondary school. This highlights the importance of 'getting it right' at primary school. Much attention has been paid to secondary schools, the first port of call for OFSTED-trained inspectors and the first target for league tables. The research evidence, however, implies that it is too late to leave effectiveness until secondary school. The academic building blocks must be in place during the primary years.

Schools' effectiveness for different pupils and those taking different subjects

Some students of different ethnic or social class backgrounds or prior attainment levels tend to do better than others within certain schools. Some departments are also more effective than others in promoting better results. This suggests that the overall concept of effective versus ineffective schools may he too simplistic to describe the dimensionality of schools' effects and has led to more detailed study of departmental effectiveness in secondary schools (Sammons et al., 1994).

Context specificity of school effectiveness

It has become increasingly clear that what works in one context may lack relevance in others. This has been found in studies of schools serving students from different social class backgrounds and in international attempts to replicate one country's findings elsewhere or examine the same factors. This has implications for generalizability of research findings.

School improvement: definition and aims

The goals of school improvement have begun to move closer to those of school effectiveness as the importance of student outcomes is increasingly acknowledged. The most frequently quoted definition emanates from the International School Improvement Project (ISIP):

a systematic sustained effort aimed at change in learning conditions and other related internal conditions in one or more schools with the ultimate aim of accomplishing educational goals more effectively.

(van Velzen et al., 1985)

This definition highlights the importance of careful planning management and continuity even in the face of difficulties. It also emphasizes a teaching and learning focus as well as the need for supporting organizational conditions. Additionally, the intricate relationship between school improvement and change is highlighted.

Indeed, all school improvement involves change, although it cannot be assumed that all change leads to improvement. A more recent definition of improvement views it as 'a distinct approach to educational change that enhances student outcomes as well as strengthening the school's capacity for managing change' (Hopkins et al., 1994).

Research on school improvement

In the 1960s 'school improvement' innovations from outside were frequently introduced to schools in a top-down manner. The original targets were organization and curriculum, with pupil-oriented outcomes as the goal. Lack of teacher commitment to this approach, however, led to a new improvement paradigm in the 1980s. This celebrated a 'bottom-up' approach through the use of practitioner rather than external knowledge, and the focus shifted from the school to the teacher, although the improvement attempt was 'whole-school' oriented. School self-evaluation or school-based review was emphasized, as the movement shifted in orientation towards the process of change. The outcomes of schooling, once accepted as given, became open to debate. This process-oriented 'journey', however, did not always lead to actual improvement in students' achievement and, by the late-1980s, there began to be a return towards a focus on the evaluation of processes and outcomes.

The 1990s have seen a further movement in this direction, exemplified in the approach of the Improving the Quality of Education for All (IQEA) project at the University of Cambridge Institute of Education (Hopkins et al., 1994) that involves measurement of pupil outcomes but is chiefly concerned with the classroom and school-level processes that lead to such outcomes.

The improvement strategies also blend the research and practitioner knowledge that has come to be associated with the school improvement movement, but with a greater emphasis on working *with* rather than *on* schools.

The process and outcomes of improvement

School improvement essentially involves change. Most researchers have described three broad change process phases. The first, *initiation*, incorporates the process that leads up to the decision to change. The second, *implementation*, consists of early experiences of putting innovations into practice. The third, *institutionalization*, describes whether or not innovations are embedded into ongoing practice. A fourth state, *outcome*, refers to a variety of results, including the impact on students, teachers, the organization and school–community relations (Fullan, 1991). Generally, these outcomes focus on the extent of improvement measured according to specified criteria.

The actual process of improvement has been described as the determination, by the school, of priorities which are then formulated within a coherent strategy. Once underway, problems tend to arise that lead to resistance or 'internal turbulence'. This causes a slowing down of progress and frustration that often leads to abandonment of the original priority in favour of a new one. Change is notoriously 'messy' and time-consuming. When faced with problems, however, people in 'moving' schools respond by adapting internal teaching, learning and organizational conditions. This changes the school's culture and enables them to surmount the difficulties.

Characteristics of the innovation, individuals and organization

Superficial solutions or 'bandwagons' have been demonstrated not to work or to lead to unnecessary overload. Successful innovations meet a need, are clear, complex and of high quality. Essentially, a change has to be worth the effort. Change also rarely involves single innovations. Rather, several ideas and activities are involved simultaneously. The skill lies in the ability to weave the various activities into a coherent whole (Stoll and Fink, 1996).

Various individual and organizational factors have also been demonstrated to be influential and to determine the school's readiness for change. These include the innovation's compatibility with the school's culture, increasingly recognized as a fundamental influence on school improvement. Teachers' concerns, interests, needs and skills are also important, as well as their psychological states.

Routes to improvement

There has been a reluctance to offer 'hard-and-fast' rules for school improvement, because of schools' individual contexts and cultures. Joyce (1991) described five different 'doors' offered by proponents of school improvement. We have updated this metaphor to look at current improvement doors being opened in Britain. Some of these doors are being opened from *inside*.

- Collegiality – the development of cohesive and professional relations within and beyond schools, and efforts to improve culture.
- Research – study and use of research findings on school and classroom effectiveness and school improvement.
- Self-evaluation – the collection and analysis of school and pupil data, action research in classrooms and appraisal.
- Curriculum – the introduction of self-chosen curricular or cross-curricular changes or projects.
- Teaching and learning – the study, discussion and development of teaching skills and strategies. Examples include flexible learning and cooperative group work initiatives.
- Partnerships – activities and projects that involve parents, community representatives and agencies, local education authorities, business, industry, higher education, TECs and educational consultants among others.

● School development planning.

Other doors are opened by those *outside* the school.

● Inspection – after a visit by an inspection team, schools are expected to generate actions to address highlighted improvement areas.
● Provision of 'value-added' data – linked with league tables, the local education authority and/or higher education staff adjust assessment information to take account of prior attainment and background factors. This enables schools to see to what extent they have boosted pupils' progress.
● External projects – similar to partnerships, except the impetus for change comes from outside (e.g. a project led by the local education authority).
● Quality approaches – emanating from business and industry, approaches include Total Quality Management (TQM) and Investors In People.
● National Curriculum and associated assessments – the assumption is that the need to master subjects promotes curriculum development and practical experience of administering assessments creates understanding of, and new ideas for, assessment.

Joyce argues that adherence to one approach alone is inadequate and that major school improvement efforts need to open all internal doors. The reality of the 1990s suggests that many external doors are also opened. The opening any of these doors, however, without attention to the deeper culture and organizational conditions of the school, is unlikely to lead to real improvement.

A report commissioned for OFSTED found 60 urban school improvement projects around England (Barber et al., 1995). These projects vary in their approach and can be seen to open different doors. Some have a specific curriculum focus (e.g. Impact Mathematics in Haringey LEA and the City Reading Project in Oxford LEA). Others have origins in data collection and analysis, including work in many local education authorities (e.g. Nottinghamshire, Shropshire and Suffolk). A door opened by many of the survey respondents was improvement through partnership (e.g. Business Compacts in Cleveland and Enfield and Barnet, the Middlesborough Community Education Project and Parental Involvement in the Core Curriculum in Tower Hamlets).

One approach that offers the opportunity of opening all doors simultaneously is the school-based development process. There are many varieties of this model that has its British origins in school self-review and is now exemplified in *school development planning*. A prototype for many others was *Guidelines for Review and Internal Development in Schools* (GRIDS) (McMahon et al., 1984). This was a voluntary process which schools were encouraged to adapt. Its focus was on review, leading to development for improvements and the review was for internal use, rather than external accountability. The process was also directed at the whole school rather than individual teachers or small groups. Subsequent models throughout the world have followed a broadly similar format, although some have now become mandatory and accountability-linked. Unlike many of the other doors, the process provides an improvement strategy that includes an audit of needs, setting of priorities, means for implementation and evaluation.

Factors identified by school effectiveness and school improvement

While it is acknowledged that no simple combination of factors produces an effective school, several reviewers have identified certain common processes and characteristics of more effective schools and those seen to have improved. In a recent review, British and North American research literature has been summarized and a list provided of key factors or correlates of effectiveness (Sammons et al., 1995). These are neither exhaustive, nor are they necessarily independent of each other. They offer, however, a useful summary of the most common factors that have been found to be associated with effective schools. Such factors provide a picture of what an effective school looks like. What they cannot explain, however, is *how* the school became effective. This is the domain of school improvement. Despite the differences in approach and orientation of the two fields, their findings are, for the most part, complementary. We have adapted Sammons's factors slightly to incorporate the factors that have been identified as leading to school improvement. While the school

Table 1

Complementary factors for school effectiveness and improvement

	SCHOOL EFFECTIVENESS *(the final picture)*	SCHOOL IMPROVEMENT *(facilitating conditions)*
1. PARTICIPATORY LEADERSHIP	• Firm and purposeful • A participative approach • The leading professional	• Headteacher as motivator and guide • Teacher involvement in leadership roles and decision-making • Teachers as change agents
2. SHARED VISION AND GOALS	• Unity of purpose • Consistent practice	• Vision building • Use of evolutionary planning process • Working for the whole school's good
3. TEAMWORK	• Collegiality and collaboration	• Teacher involvement and empowerment • Opportunities for collaboration and collegiality
4. A LEARNING ENVIRONMENT	• An orderly atmosphere • An attractive working environment	• Orderly and secure environment • A positive ethos • A place where 'risk taking' is encouraged
5. EMPHASIS ON TEACHING AND LEARNING	• Maximum learning time • Academic emphasis • Achievement focus • Efficient organisation • Clarity of purpose • Structured lessons • Adaptive practice	• A focus central to teachers' and pupils' concerns • Varied and appropriate repertoire • Teachers learning and practising new strategies

effectiveness factors represent a snapshot of what one would see in an effective school, the school improvement 'factors' or conditions are worked on as part of an overall change strategy or route.

	SCHOOL EFFECTIVENESS *(the final picture)*	SCHOOL IMPROVEMENT *(facilitating conditions)*
6. **HIGH EXPECTATIONS**	• High expectations for all • Expectations communicated • Intellectual challenge	• High expectations about adults and pupils • Aspirations and success criteria shared
7. **POSITIVE REINFORCEMENT**	• Clear and fair discipline • Feedback	• Behaviour policy maintained and monitored • Celebration • Appreciation and recognition of teachers • Capturing teacher enthusiasm
8. **MONITORING AND ENQUIRY**	• Monitoring pupil performance • Evaluating school performance	• Setting, monitoring and evaluating success criteria • Classroom research techniques used by teachers • Ongoing review and necessary adaptation
9. **PUPIL RIGHTS AND RESPONSIBILITIES**	• High pupil self-esteem • Positions of responsibility • Control of work	• Involvement of pupils in management of learning • Eliciting pupils' views
10. **LEARNING FOR ALL**	• School-based staff development	• Teachers as continuing learners • Coaching and mentoring • Peer observation and feedback • 'Critical friendships'
11. **PARTNERSHIPS AND SUPPORT**	• Parental involvement	• Schemes to involve parents and community • External support • Developing networks and clusters

Resources

Much school effectiveness and school improvement literature ignores the question of resources. This is because, in a number of cases, schools included in any sample have similar levels of funding and – as a result – there is too little variability to distinguish between them on this dimension. This should not be taken as proof that resource levels are not important, although such an argument has been robustly presented by at least one American educational economist (Hanushek, 1986). A more common view among British researchers is that resources help, but do not guarantee effectiveness. There is little support for the view that reducing levels of funding will improve the performance of pupils, teachers or schools. One area in which resource levels have been widely debated is that of class size.

Current research and development activities

Given the complementarity of the factors identified by school effectiveness and school improvement, it is perhaps surprising that, until recently, in Britain there has been an 'intellectually and practically unhealthy' reluctance between the two communities to join forces (Reynolds et al., 1993). In contrast, in North America, practitioners and policy-makers have worked with researchers to draw on research from both traditions and link the two areas through improvement efforts. In 1988, schools in almost half of the school districts in the US (approximately 6,500) were engaged in such projects. The last few years, however, have seen a change in Britain, with a range of research and development activities deliberately established to bridge the divide. These encompass action research projects, networks, courses, indicator development and analysis, support material and centres.

Action research projects

Many of the urban improvement projects outlined in the report commissioned by OFSTED attempt to evaluate outcomes as well as processes. Three such examples are Sheffield's Raising Achievement and Participation project, Hammersmith and Fulham LEA's Schools Make a Difference (SMAD) project (Myers, forthcoming), and the Lewisham School Improvement project, a partnership between Lewisham schools, the local education authority and the Institute of Education at London University (Stoll and Thomson, forthcoming). A different kind of project is the Improving School Effectiveness project, funded by the Scottish Office Education Department (MacBeath and Mortimore, 1994). A team of researchers from Strathclyde University and the Institute of Education are following 60 schools (primary and secondary) to ascertain the value added to a range of pupil outcomes. At the same time, 24 of these schools are supported in improvement efforts in three areas:

1. school development planning
2. teaching and learning
3. the development of a 'moving school' ethos.

These processes will be monitored in more depth.

Networks

A variety of national and local networks have been started around Britain. The School Improvement Network at the Institute of Education has been created to enable educators throughout Britain to share experiences and ideas, discuss common difficulties, reflect on fundamental issues related to school improvements and access important research findings which can be translated into practice. Members receive newsletters, research summaries and a contact list. They can also attend meetings. Other school improvement networks are operated by Dorset LEA and Bretton Hall in Wakefield. A network for school effectiveness and improvement researchers was funded by the ESRC and now meets twice a year.

Courses

The Institutes of Education at London and Cambridge Universities and Birmingham and Bath Universities offer accreditation for practitioners involved in school effectiveness and improvement initiatives.

Specifically designed higher degree courses are also available in certain universities for what has become an increasingly popular field of study.

Indicator development and analysis

Value-added analyses services are provided by several universities (particularly the Institute of Education in London and the Universities of Newcastle and Sheffield) and local education authorities to help schools examine academic results and, in some cases, students' attitudes in context. Attitude surveys have also been developed by the University of Keele, the National Foundation for Educational Research and the Scottish Office Education Department, to help schools gather baseline information from students and parents.

Resources

Several guidelines, videos and resource packs have been produced on various aspects of school improvement.[1]

Centres

A Centre for School Improvement has been established at Bath University. Activities include seminars, school-specific school improvement audits and development consultancy, work with school clusters and summer workshops. The International School Effectiveness and Improvement Centre (ISEIC) at the Institute of Education aims to draw on, extend and link the school effectiveness and improvement knowledge by engaging in:

● developmental work and action research with schools engaged in effectiveness and improvement projects

● research, in collaboration with a variety of partners including other higher education institutions, local education authority personnel, educational consultants and government agencies.

Future needs

Despite these positive ventures, many challenges still face those involved in school effectiveness and school improvement. It is well known that successful change is not a speedy process and realism about what schools may be able to achieve in one year is necessary. For pupils, however, the time they have at school is the only time for them. It is of the utmost importance, therefore, to determine any ways in which improvement can be accelerated. While hardly any studies have demonstrated improvement in the space of months rather than years, some programmes have shown remarkable success. Considerable gains in reading, for example, have been demonstrated at primary level over a one-year period, using Reading Recovery (Hobsbaum and Hillman, 1994) and at secondary levels, GCSE results in science and mathematics have also increased considerably as a result of Cognitive Acceleration Through Science (Adey and Shayer, 1994). In the US, the Success for All programme has led to significant improvements and lasting effects in reading achievement and fewer pupils being 'kept down' for another year or referred for special educational support (Slavin et al., 1994). These are only three of several methods that appear to have a powerful impact on achievement in a short time. Further work is needed urgently to identify strategies which can speed up the improvement process.

Although some school effectiveness studies have focused on the classroom, until very recently the orientation was directed much more towards school-level factors associated with effectiveness. Similarly, since the 1970s, school improvement has tended to pay greater attention to school-level processes. Recent school effectiveness studies, however, argue that most of the variation among pupils is due to classroom variation. It is clear, therefore, that school and classroom development need to be linked. One key implication is that teachers need to take a 'classroom exceeding perspective' (MacGilchrist et al., 1995), while at the same time the headteacher needs a 'classroom perceiving perspective'. Another is the need to examine how classroom and whole-school strategies are linked.

Studies of school effectiveness and improvement projects internationally demonstrate increasing agreement on the processes necessary for successful school improvement. One fundamental idea is that improvement should come from within, even if outside change agents are involved in supporting change. This requires people within the school to take charge of the change process. It has become apparent from improvement efforts over the last few years that this approach works well for the 'moving' schools or even average schools that display readiness for change. It is less successful, however, with struggling schools or, particularly, with schools in crisis. For these, more direct intervention may be necessary. Further research and case studies are needed to determine steps which may help a struggling school improve.

There is still inadequate theory to underpin our knowledge of what makes schools effective and how they improve. In particular, the interconnection between school and classroom improvement is not well described, and a better understanding of the impact of the school's context and its readiness for change is needed.

In Britain, the word 'schooling' is usually used to denote education within the ages 5–16. For effectiveness and improvement, such cut-off points are unhelpful. It is important to stress that these concepts relate to all academic institutions, including nurseries, post-16 colleges, universities and, indeed, institutes catering for adult continuing learners.

All the issues we have raised point to the need for further case studies and large-scale intervention studies of effectiveness and improvement. We think it is particularly important to attempt improvement in struggling schools, with a focus on classroom strategies and at how these are related to schools' organization and management. These case studies need to be carried out in all phases, in a variety of contexts and to incorporate measurement of a range of outcomes.

Note

[1] For a list of resources and a more detailed school effectiveness and school improvement bibliography, contact the School Improvement Network, Institute of Education, 20 Bedford Way, London WC1H OAL. Telephone: 0171 619 6347.

2 The rise of the school effectiveness movement

Lynn Davies

Introduction

This chapter looks at the implications for school management of the school effectiveness 'movement'. Traditionally, the fields of educational management and school effectiveness have occupied different camps. The former had its origins in a theoretical translation of organizational management; the latter in a sociological and empirical quest for determining the relative influence of 'family background' in children's achievement. However, there are signs that the two traditions are coming together. The international focus on 'quality' rather than just 'quantity' in education means renewed emphasis on school processes. At the same time, the demands for accountability and desires by governments to blame education for economic decline lead to pressure to expose and compare school 'outcomes'. Hence, the language of effectiveness research – input/output, process variables, value-added – is increasingly being found in management training. What used to be an American tradition, and then European, is being spread to all parts of the world. There is an international journal *School Effectiveness and School Improvement* and an annual international conference. During the 1990s there have been national conferences on effectiveness in countries such as South Africa, Botswana and Zimbabwe (Jansen, 1995); sub-Saharan Africa in general is the focus of many World Bank initiatives to translate school effectiveness research into school improvement (Development of African Education, 1995).

Admittedly, there are complaints that school effectiveness research is 'weak' on management and organization factors, focusing as it does on broad questions of 'climate' (Reynolds and Cuttance, 1992); but certain management indicators can be and are being extracted. As Cuban pointed out:

> In the surest test of popularity, the vocabulary of effective school research has entered the daily language of school administrators: high expectations; an orderly environment; a positive climate; and consensus over academic goals echo a trendy jargon . . . unlike the way things happen in fairy tales, school reform requires more than a kiss to convert a frog into a stunning prince . . . productive schooling entails more than raising test scores.
>
> (Cuban, 1984: 130–1)

It is time, therefore, to take a critical look at this effectiveness research and its potential impact on management language. In this chapter I will briefly review some of the relevant findings of the effectiveness research and consider the problems of its growth at a number of levels.

How does it work?

The premise is quite a simple one. Starting with a concern about differences in the outcomes of schooling (usually in pupil achievement), the idea is that one can establish how much of that difference is because of school-based 'factors', and then identify those factors which are linked to higher achievement. While nearly 30 years of this research have not managed to dispel Coleman's (1966) initial findings that a large proportion of divergence in pupil achievement is linked to their home enviroment, the quest is on to find those school-based things which do make a difference at the margin. Implicit is the equity concern that if only we could nail down what makes one school slightly more successful than its neighbour (although with similar children), we could expand on this knowledge to start to enable education to truly 'compensate' for society.

The methodology of research is, therefore, conceptually simple if statistically complex. The now conventional method is to establish a number of 'outcomes' or 'indicators' on which the performance of schools can be measured; control for all the intervening variables which influence that performance; and to extract the surplus, the added value (i.e. what can only be because of the school itself). An output such as pupil performance on a test is compared; contributory factors such as pupil home background, measured intelligence or previous experience are accounted for; and a league table of schools drawn up according to which school appears to do better with the same material. From this, begins the search for correlations. What factors in the 'good' schools distinguish them from the 'poor' schools? Are patterns discernible? Do these features 'cause' the better achievement?

It is a similar sort of methodology to traditional leadership theory: you identify a 'good' leader and say what goes with it. There is recognition now that much leadership theory is suspect because of the uncontested initial value judgement about who constituted the 'leaders' (white males) and then who amongst those were 'good' leaders (strong, white, heterosexual males). However, such suspicion has not always been applied to the identification of a 'good' school. We shall return to this cultural and political question later. Meanwhile, the publications on effectiveness research can generate lists of common factors in effective schooling which have international appeal.

Factors in effective schooling

What is defined as a 'good' school will clearly condition the associated factors. Inevitably, and because the ideology of the research is the systematic comparison of schools, the outcomes are usually the directly measurable indicators: assessment results, truancy rates, drop-out rates or wider delinquency by pupils as counted by number of court appearances.

The key indicator is the first of these: external examinations, specially devised tests or reading score results. The internal factors associated with good schools measured on these outcomes are often much less statistically measurable, but recognizable nonetheless; the discrepancies between various studies come with the number of headings employed and which factors come under which headings. A typical American set could be taken from Levine and Lezotte's characteristics from *Unusually Effective Schools* (1990):

- productive school climate and culture (e.g. orderly environment, staff cohesion and problem-solving orientation)
- focus on student acquisition of knowledge (e.g. maximum time and mastery of skills)
- appropriate monitoring of student progess
- practice-oriented staff development at the school site
- outstanding leadership (e.g. high expenditure of time and energy, support for teachers)
- salient parent involvement
- effective instructional arrangements and implementation (e.g. grouping, pacing and materials)
- high operationalized expectations and requirements for students
- student sense of efficacy
- multicultural instruction and sensitivity
- rigorous and equitable student promotions policies.

Yet even with these extensive headings, it is apparent that categorization is problematic. Is the fostering of collective goals a leadership question or a climate question? Is the provision of rewards and feedback a curriculum question or an organizational question? When factors are identified, the headings they are put under by researchers becomes not just a technical issue: the headings will signify who is seen to take responsibility for these, whether the leadership or the collective. In the end, is not everything 'climate'?

Most effectiveness research has been in the US, Europe and Australia.

There are fewer statistically grounded studies in developing countries. Those larger ones that are there are financed almost exclusively by the World Bank. One interesting more qualitative example was Vulliamy's research in Papua New Guinea (1987), where high schools were compared on their performance rating matched against examination scores of their intake. The list of factors characterizing the good schools had similar features to the above, but with more emphasis on facilities and staffing, that is, elements not directly controllable by the head. The qualifications of the staff, teacher pay and housing, water, electricity, toilets, the presence or absence of a spirit duplicator – all had correlations with the school rating. Similar findings about the impact of teacher salaries, incentives and qualifications as well as availability of curriculum materials emerged in Tanzania (Omari and Mosha, 1987). The stark differences between schools in terms of their resourcing in developing countries may be one of the reasons why greater 'school effects' are found there than in richer countries. In establishing what makes better 'investments' in schools, the reviews of all the statistical studies of developing countries up to the mid-1990s show that 'the single most important finding ... is the significance of textbooks and other "material inputs" in explaining school achievement' (Jansen, 1995).

If we are interested in the school effectiveness research from a management point of view, we need however to go back to the research to select the factors *specifically controllable by management*. A combined list from First and Third World literature might be:

1. combination of firm leadership and a decision-making process where teachers feel their views are represented

2. ample use of rewards, praise and appreciation for both students and staff

3. opportunity for students to take responsibility in the running of the school

4. low rates of punishment

5. care of the school environment, buildings and working conditions

6. clear goals (possibly written) and incorporation (not coercion) of students and parents into acceptance of these goals

7. high expectations and feedback

8. teachers as good role models (time-keeping, willingness to deal with pupil problems, lesson preparation and maximum communication with the pupils)

9. clearly delegated duties to teachers and students

10. consistent record-keeping and monitoring (not necessarily testing)

11. vigorous selection and replacement of staff

12. maverick orientation, ingenuity in acquiring resources and risk-taking by heads

13. heads 'buffering' schools from negative external influences

14. convincing teachers they *do* make a difference to children's lives

15. good external relations to aid financial and moral support for the school

16. avoidance of nepotism and favouritism.

The positive features of school effectiveness research are then that they avoid the pessimism that *everything* is determined by student and resource 'input' factors, that is, that the combination of the background and ability of students and the level of material resourcing of the school will be the best predictors of school success or failure. Levin and Lockheed's (1993) collection *Effective Schools in Developing Countries* found schools who were able to provide the necessary instructional inputs despite otherwise impoverished circumstances. The above 'management-controllable' list does not necessarily cost any more money and begins to show what *can* be changed in school management. Harris et al. (1996) are able to put together effectiveness findings with OFSTED criteria to present a model for school management based on the development of a 'learning culture'. Indeed, it might be argued that (after pupil background) management is the key issue – some studies show that curriculum innovation and new materials make no difference to students' actual achievement! The list appears to provide clear guidelines to principals to tackle immediately the key organizational and climate factors associated with 'better' schools.

Problems with 'effectiveness' ideologies

However, there are a number of grave problems with the school effectiveness research and its usage. These appear at different levels and stages.

Outcome measures

It will have become apparent that the selection of the outcomes by which to compare schools is not a neutral activity. A tendency to select 'the measurable' leads to a focus on examination and test results. The implication is that we all agree that the school's prime task is to get as many children through examinations as possible. All the other possible goals of the school – citizenship, self-esteem, political awareness, social responsibility, caring human beings, solidarity and cooperation, vocational preparation and life-long learning – are sidelined. Clearly, it is more difficult to evaluate such longer-term effects, but the problem is that after a while in the discussion of effectiveness variables we begin to forget that they were gained on a very narrow range of outcome indicators or there is the unproven assumption that what is good for competitive or individualized tests will also be good for cooperative or social learning. It may or may not be, but it is highly dangerous to embark on a school improvement programme based on effectiveness research unless the goals of the school exactly match the measured outcomes in the studies.

The narrowness of 'measurable outcomes' is, therefore, also a cultural problem. A country such as Tanzania might have as its prime goal for education that of self-reliance; for Papua New Guinea it might be a practical use of school curriculum to help the community. It *could* be that 'firm leadership' or a 'democratic' school climate are helpful both to academic orientations and self-reliant ones; but we need to know this empirically from research in schools with different goals. In Tanzania, Lwehabura (1993) compared 'non-conventional' schools in terms of their success in self-reliant activities and pointed to features such as the presence of active schools councils and teachers happily joining in agricultural activities as distinctive features. Not just the factors themselves, but how 'firm leadership' or 'democracy' would be interpreted in different cultures needs unpacking. This has been explored by Harber (1995) and Davies (1995).

Technical problems

School effectiveness researchers will be the first to point out the technical and statistical difficulties in drawing firm conclusions about an 'ideal school'. They have found that there can be differences in the effects:

- in different geographical areas
- for different subjects in the curriculum
- for different ages of pupil
- for girls and boys
- for high achieving children and low achieving children
- for different sorts of learning.

A management practice associated with good scores for rote memory in geography by 10-year old boys in UK may be ineffective for conceptual learning of mathematics by 16-year-old girls in France.

One of the reasons for such inconsistency is that in any one school environment all the factors interact. While the research has been geared into *isolating* variables, in reality they all affect each other and work in tandem or indeed in contradiction. At a broad level, the factors appear generalizable and indisputable: no-one would *not* want to have 'a good and pleasant school climate conducive to learning'. It is when we start to break down what is 'conducive to learning' that contradictions appear. For an older student, conducive may mean opportunity for self-directed learning; for a younger student conducive means firm structuring by the teacher. Even then, whether self-directed learning is effective will depend on other variables such as library provision and flexible timetabling; within the 'climate' category itself, it will depend on the particular way feedback is interpeted and used by different members of staff. It comes as no surprise then that the same achievements can be arrived at by contrasting methods and combinations of factors or, conversely, that a school trying to emulate another's 'factors' may achieve disappointing results. Gonakelle School in Sri Lanka, for example, flourished through increasing the number of teachers required to stay for three years, combined with parental support; yet the researchers stress the significance of local factors and timing, rather than the applicability of variables derived from very different material and cultural situations (Little and Sivasithambaran, 1993).

The fundamental technical question in effectiveness research thus becomes the *causal* one. Certain factors may be *associated* with good performance; but this is not to say that they *cause* them. A good school may be found to have high expectations of its students; but those high expectations may be a *result* of having a good student intake over a number of years who are likely to produce good results. It would be difficult *not* to have high expectations; nor are those expectations the result of a deliberate management strategy. A school with low achieving students who suddenly decided on the basis of the research evidence to raise their expectations of students may be disappointed to see no dramatic improvement and may encounter a degree of cynicism from students and staff. Some studies in UK showed effective schools to be housed in older, more cramped buildings. This does not mean that the buildings *helped* in the effectiveness, still less that governments should stop spending money on buildings. In this instance, the buildings were in turn associated with other factors: the effective schools in this locality were the ones with longer traditions and loyalties which inspired a sense of ownership. Elsewhere, and particularly in developing countries, the buildings do become crucial as they represent the difference between learning under a roof and learning in the open air subject to the heat of the sun, the rain or intrusions by local cattle.

Interpretations

How do practitioners translate school effectiveness research into school improvement? They will immediately spot the confusion over language. An 'indicator of effectiveness' can be used to mean both an *outcome* – what the school is directly aiming to attain – and a *factor* – a means thought to help arrive at that outcome. Thus, lists of indicators can include both something like 'high reading scores' and 'class libraries'. Admittedly, 'good community links' could be both a goal in its own right and a factor in pupil achievement; yet it is particularly in the area of management that there can be dangers of confusing goals and factors. 'Firm leadership' is not a goal in itself, it is merely a possible means towards the main purposes of the educational enterprise, such as pupil learning. If we focus on the factors alone, without continuously evaluating how and why they might lead to better learning, then 'good management' starts to take on a life of its own and the managers assume vastly more importance than is advisable.

Good schools may have a mission statement, but this does not mean that the preparation of a mission statement is sufficient in itself. Because the level of management training may be associated with more effective schools, there are trainees (and trainers!) who assume that it is enough to have been on the course. The question in the forefront of our minds however should be how exactly a mission statement, a management training course or a change in delegation would promote student learning in the ways desired. 'Factors' and 'process indicators' are only intermediaries, simply clues to help us experiment with different means. As the Association for the Development of African Education acknowledges:

> it is not the 'right mix' of inputs which will lead by itself to changes in student performance but rather the educational process in individual schools which determines how effective the inputs will be for pupils' learning. The effectiveness of schools is seen not to lie in the specific list of discrete additive elements, but in the creation of a whole efficient working system, which includes its people, structure, relationships, ideologies, goals, intellectual substance, motivation and will.
>
> (DAE 1995: 2)

My view is that changing that 'system' would require a very clear commitment to learning as the prime goal, a broad but agreed concept of what is to be learned, but flexibility and experimentation in the means to get there. A rigid commitment to flexibility, perhaps.

Explaining the ineffective school

When we look at the lists of factors associated with effective schools, there are few surprises. Many of them appear to be common sense – efficient use of classroom time, moral support for teachers and reviewing and monitoring progress. Others are no more than circular statements – a good school is one that is managed well, a school with high standards of behaviour has a good discipline pattern. The surprise is not in the factors, but in why all schools and all managers do not adhere to them. Presumably, all heads would in theory see it wise to confront problems tactfully, to have clear job descriptions or for everyone to use their time efficiently. The effectiveness research does not tell us much that we do not already know and that we would not adhere to in principle. Comparisons may well identify ineffective schools but the factorial analysis does not tell us the human motivations and interpretations that prevent operationalizing what appears to be 'common sense'.

For that, we have to go back to the 'realities' research (Davies, 1994, Chapter 2). Teachers and heads may acknowledge at one level that teacher punctuality for classes will act as a good role model for students' own commitment to the classroom process; yet, in some schools, teachers consistently arrive after the children or keep them waiting in corridors. Why? It may be a number of things. It may be technical problems of teachers having to move between school buildings on different sites, but it may also be a symptom of low motivation which keeps teachers in the staffroom until the last possible minute. Or it may be a particular interpretation of the role of authority: a teacher may believe that there can be different rules for teachers and taught, and that children should do as they say, not as they do. They may believe that it is all right for teachers to be late, but not for students. Indeed, teachers may see it as promoting their authority to sweep into a classroom later than the pupils; a sign of control is the power to make others wait for you.

This example demonstrates the intricate connection between a particular teacher or management action and the surrounding culture. For a head to start tightening up on teacher punctuality may be pointless unless that head has engaged with the basic value systems of the staff. The reason why teacher punctuality is implicated in effectiveness in some schools is because it is part of a whole ethos which gives equal respect to students' rights. It would be part of an ethos which tried to have similar conduct rules for teachers and taught, and where teachers prioritized students' learning time over their own needs to exert power. Trying to impose punctuality in a value system where teachers felt uncomfortable about students' rights to learn or to have similar codes of conduct to the teachers would simply mean teachers finding other ways to maintain distance (e.g. arriving on time but then spending ten minutes insisting on the students sitting to attention).

Effectiveness research on its own will not explain ineffective schools, nor can the findings be tacked on piecemeal to the management structure and ethos of those ineffective schools. Fuller and Clarke critique the 'policy mechanics' who:

> seek universal remedies that can be manipulated by central agencies and assume that the same instructional materials and pedagogical practices hold constant meaning in the eyes of teachers and children from diverse cultural settings.
>
> (Fuller and Clarke, 1994: 119)

The hardest part for policy-makers has been the attempt to turn school effectiveness into school improvement. The power of the inhabitants to interpret and subvert their world is one key reason for this. In effectiveness research, however, power relations are ignored. As Angus pointed out in a key review of effectiveness ideology, 'practice is [seen as] imposed rather than constructed, negotiated or asserted; it is a set of techniques to be employed by teacher technicians on malleable pupils' (Angus, 1993: 331).

Lack of a political analysis

More significant still than the lack of a micropolitical analysis is the deeper flaw in effectiveness research: the lack of a macropolitical consideration of the function of schooling within what Fuller (1991) would term a 'fragile State'. How does socialization through mass schooling support shaky economies and political regimes? School effectiveness however is concerned with 'what works'. It does not concern itself with the question of in whose interests it works. In the focus on assessment or behavioural outcomes there is no critique of the knowledge and cultural base to these definitions of 'achievement'. The possibility that schools and their curricula can be organized in the interests of the ruling class, of males or of the dominant ethnic group is ignored.

> Family background, social class, any notion of context, are typically regarded as 'noise' – as 'outside' background factors which must be controlled for and then stripped away so that the researcher can concentrate on the important domain of school factors.
>
> (Angus, 1993:341)

The school's essentially non-educational role as a sifting, sorting and labelling agency is played down in favour of some vision that all schools could become effective. Yet for schooling to fulfil its selection role it is necessary for a proportion of students (or even schools) to 'fail'. Education then can help to legitimize the inequalities in society by attributing them to qualifications and credentials gained in the formal system. There is no point in having examinations if everyone passes them. So even if the adoption of effectiveness techniques meant larger numbers of children gaining good examination results, this does not in itself tackle the ensuing 'qualification inflation'.

Effectiveness research is generally popular with governments. The emphasis on schooling making a difference justifies the spending and draws attention away from structured inequalities in society (Davies, 1996). The continuation of the discovery that schools apparently differ in their ability to provide opportunity (however marginal the difference) plays into the hands of those who would see it as convenient to blame education and teachers for society's ills. If some schools can succeed, why can't you all? The choice of the measurable outputs as the 'key' indicators of a school's success supports a factory model of schooling, with only technical improvements needed to increase production. Until such time as we have research which systematically compares schools on their ability to produce critically aware, politicized citizens, all that the effectiveness research does at present is substantiate the mythology that with a bit of sharpening up of the teaching profession and their managers, education systems could reduce inequality, provide universal opportunity and boost declining economies.

Critical implications

What then can we salvage from the appealing, but sometimes suspect, effectiveness research? Not abandonment, certainly – it is not that we do not want our schools to be effective. Not a quantitative refinement of methodology, better and more sophisticated statistics and multivariate analysis. Instead, the way forward is for a much more politicized exploration of the various definitions of 'effective', and who controls contemporary interpretations. One interesting Australian study *Making Schools More Effective* (McGaw et al., 1992) distributed booklets and questionnaires to a huge sample of school participants and other interested people, asking them to report on their perceptions and expectations of schools. School communities from around Australia gave the message that they wanted schools that stimulated intellectual development by setting high, but realistic expectations. But they also wanted schools that developed students' personal and social skills. Above all, they wanted schools in which students learned to think well of themselves, to develop a sense of personal value and a confidence in themselves to take with them to adult life. They wanted competition, but they wanted it to be with a student's own past performance, not with the the performances of other students. Performance on tests of basic skills was rarely mentioned; student assessment was not seen as a major contributor to school effectiveness. It was the *qualitative* aspects which were of most concern to school communities.

Similar voices are starting to be heard in UK with regard to government testing of pupils. The right wing rationale was for accountability to parents, with league tables of schools giving parents the information they needed to make choices for their children. When asked, however, the majority of parents wanted the proposed tests scrapped, supporting the teachers in seeing them as taking time from the real business of learning and causing individual stress to children.

The message is clear. Rather than governments or teams of outside researchers coming into schools and classifying them on their outputs and processes, school communities must themselves investigate what constitutes effectiveness for all the participants – most crucially the students. Effectiveness studies often dehumanize students by reducing them to 'intake variables'; there is a cultural deficit, a stereotyped approach which appears to sympathize with schools for the 'poor quality' of their intake. But asking the 'intake' what they want and expect from school will allow the cultural and background differences between pupils to emerge as important and rich data which should begin to shape what and whom the school is for.

The implications for transparent management are to conduct one's own effectiveness research. The 'outcomes' must be identified by the school community itself. The comparisons on performance on those outcomes must be internal to that institution over time or mutually agreed between institutions. The collection of data must be a joint enterprise by all participants. It may well be that some of the managerial factors identified earlier will start to emerge. Whatever the definition of 'effectiveness', whether student self-esteem, social responsibility or knowledge of family planning techniques, it is likely that some version of 'ample use of praise and appreciation' and 'students participating in the running of the school' will be there. But the reasons to examine, experiment with and even encourage opposition to the indicators will be home grown, rather than transplanted from government edict or an enthusiastic training course.

Jansen (1995) claims an incompatibility between the effectiveness paradigm and the quality paradigm, with a plea for a shift towards the latter. I would agree, but could nonetheless see the possibility of some syntheses. What is of value to managers in existing effectiveness research is in providing clues and in preventing having to reinvent the wheel from scratch. A school administration concerned about student discipline, for example, may be trying to make a decision between tightening up on the rules and the punishments or reforming them. Exploration of the school effectiveness literature will show that 'successful' schools appear not in fact have overly strict regimes, and work best with minimum rules agreed or suggested by students and staff. Such information gives a school encouragement to experiment with different regimes, and not feel it would be the end of civilization if students wore coloured socks. Factorial lists of good-school features should not *constrain* management development but provide a source of ideas for wider experimentation.

Nonetheless, heads and schools should not take on themselves total responsibility for affecting children's lives and careers. It must be remembered that in spite of what we know about between-school differences, the wide structures and cultures of society and the narrow range of learning experiences provided in formal education means that schools will continue to disadvantage certain groups. Schools may want to tackle head on the fact acknowledged by effectiveness research that family 'background' is still the best predictor of attainment in pyramidal education systems. Where the research can help is when it demonstrates how different levels of funding to schools in different localities and social class areas make a difference to students' achievement. While heads can indeed take on board some of the 'cost-free' implications around management style, they could also use the information on the impact of resources to keep up pressure on governments for adequate and equitable levels of funding. Used sensitively, effectiveness research can show how responsibility for the 'success' of schools must be shared at all levels of macro and micro politics.

3 Philosophical perspectives on school effectiveness and school improvement

John White

Introduction

What contribution can philosophy of education make to educational research? The question has been around now for some 30 years (Peters and White, 1969). One kind of answer can take the form of philosophical commentary on an ongoing research programme. This is the approach I adopt here. I focus on some philosophically interesting aspects of recent writings on school effectiveness and school improvement. (See also Elliott 1996, who comes to broadly similar conclusions on several of the issues raised below.) An earlier work, Barrow and Milburn (1986: 215–20), is stimulating on the related topic of teacher effectiveness.

Research on school effectiveness (SE) and on school improvement (SI) has proceeded apace in various countries in the last two decades, attracting the attention of politicians and policy-makers as well as practitioners. Among other things, SE research (SER) has concentrated on identifying the factors making schools equally matched for ability and social class of intake and other variables better than others – i.e. more effective – at achieving academic and other goals; while SI work has focused on helping schools to do better on these factors and thus more likely to meet the goals.

More specifically, SER has identified a number of factors associated with high-achieving schools in such outcomes as reading and mathematics scores and low truancy rates. These tend to include such things as participatory leadership, shared vision and goals, teamwork among staff, an orderly learning environment, an emphasis on teaching and learning, high expectations, clear and fair discipline and parental involvement. SI studies have concentrated on helping schools better to achieve these desiderata and thus to become more effective.

In what follows, I limit myself to philosophical remarks, fully aware that there are many other issues in this many-sided field.

The notion of effectiveness

I begin with problems of definition. What is meant by 'effectiveness' in this context?

It is common to think of 'effectiveness' simply in terms of means and ends. If X is effective, it is good as a means of producing outcome Y. A hammer is an effective tool for banging in nails; a screwdriver is not. Some SE literature seems to view the term in this way (Stoll and Mortimore, 1995: 1; see also Scheerens, 1992, Chapter 1). This sees effectiveness as a value-neutral term, having to do simply with causal relationships between Xs and Ys. It makes the study of effectiveness a wholly empirical matter, something solely for scientific investigation.

But *is* 'effectiveness' a value-neutral term? If we say using a hammer is an effective means of driving in a nail, the end could be good or bad – repairing the garden fence or crucifixion. Here the notion is purely causal. But 'effectiveness' also sometimes connotes more than this. When we think of the use of hammers, we often *take it for granted* that the end is desirable. In this way, effectiveness can come to be thought of as a good thing, not only from an instrumental point of view, but also more widely. There is a danger of this happening with SER, especially as its take-up by policy-makers grows. Given how natural it is to assume that schools, like hospitals, work to benign ends, whatever helps them to attain those ends more efficiently will often be seen as uncontroversially desirable. The fact that measures to make less effective schools more effective are labelled 'school *improvement*' blurs the distinction still further between 'good as a means' and 'good more generally'; as does the definition of an 'effective school' as one 'in which students *progress* further than might be expected from a consideration of its intake' (Mortimore, 1995a: 7). While both 'improvement' and 'progress'*could* be understood in a value-neutral, means-end sense, as implying getting closer to the ends in question, however good or bad these were, they usually have more global connotations.

'Effectiveness' may not always be the value-neutral term it seemed at first glance. This is important, since if the ends of SER *are* taken for granted, they may come not to be questioned.

Factors in school effectiveness

Leaving matters of definition on one side, I now focus on that part of SER which tries to find out which factors within the school are responsible for effectiveness. This is claimed to be something which has to be empirically determined. The research proceeds, in fact, by examining the strength of correlations between possible factor-variables and outcomes. Highly correlated factor-variables are not for that reason alone causally related to outcomes, but given that the same high correlations are found in research from different countries, 'the plausibility of these variables operating as mechanisms of school effectiveness has been increased by the frequency with which they have been replicated' (Mortimore, 1995b: 346). I will come back to the international aspects of the research later.

If the relationship between factors and outcomes is empirical, then we should expect to find that the two are logically distinct. In other words, if one starts from a certain outcome, it should not be possible to derive by logical argument that such and such a factor *must* have contributed to it.

On the other hand, if we do find that factors and outcomes *are* logically related in this way, then empirical investigation is otiose. To take a hackneyed, but nevertheless helpful, example: if one knows that a certain man is a bachelor, one knows that he must be unmarried. The 'must' here is a logical 'must': it follows from being a bachelor that one is unmarried, since being unmarried is part of what we mean by 'bachelor'. It is obvious here that empirical investigation is otiose. There would be no point in trying to find out about bachelor after bachelor whether they were unmarried: we know the answer already.

Are SE factors empirically determinable, as claimed? Or are there logical relationships between factors and outcomes such that empirical research would be beside the point? To answer this, we have to look more closely at factors and outcomes.

Although details vary between researchers, various factors have been identified – such things as participatory leadership, shared vision and goals, teamwork, a learning environment, high expectations and so on. The outcomes that SE work looks at focus on pupils' attainments in basic skills or in GCSE results, but can also include such things as truancy rates or self-concept scores. Are these items related empirically or logically?

Let us concentrate on academic achievements. Among the factors that lead to high attainment in this domain are:

1. an orderly learning environment

2. an emphasis on learning and teaching, bringing with it such things as an academic emphasis, an achievement focus, clarity of purpose and structured lessons.

Schools which lack 1. and 2. tend to be less effective in producing children with high scores in reading, writing, mathematics and GCSE results. How far can we work this out logically from our understanding of the outcome? How far do we need empirical research to tell it us?

That logical relationships come into the story to some extent is undeniable. Let us take factor 1., an orderly learning environment. Could the high academic scores in question come about without this? It is logically possible that a particular school class does well even though the classroom is always in chaos. The notion makes sense: it contains no logical contradiction. This might make the connection between factor and outcome look empirical.

But could classrooms *always* be in chaos and high achievements result? At this point, we approach the unintelligible. This is because of what is built into our understanding of what normally counts as successful teaching. Teaching implies intending the bringing-about of learning. For children to learn from teachers, certain conditions must – logically must – be satisfied. The learners must pass from a state of not-knowing to a state of knowing. To reach this, their teachers must draw their attention to the subject matter to be learnt and correct their mistakes so that they come to have a better understanding. This requires some sort of organized, planned activity on the part of the teacher. All this is part of what we understand by teaching. If classrooms were always in chaos, these organized teaching activities would be, by definition, ruled out. (On philosophical discussions of the concept of teaching, see Pearson, 1989, especially Chapters 6 and 7; and Scheffler, 1960, especially Chapters 4 and 5.)

If this is right, then even though high achievement in conditions of chaos were conceivable on particular occasions, it could not *normally* be like that, because of what is built into our understanding of successful teaching. Cases of high achievement in chaotic classrooms must be seen as abnormal, requiring a special explanation.

Similar points could be made about factor 2., to do with an emphasis on teaching and learning, an academic focus, clarity of purpose and structured lessons. All these things are built into the concept of successful teaching.

We do not need empirical investigations to tell us that orderly classrooms, structured lessons, etc., are conducive to high academic results. We can work this out from the understanding we already have of what it is to be a successful teacher.

The form of this argument has a long pedigree in modern philosophy of education. One of its most celebrated applications was in David Hamlyn's (1967) critique of Piaget's developmental theory. Piaget claimed to show via empirical evidence that children develop from a stage of concrete operations to a stage of formal operations. Hamlyn argued that, if we are thinking of normal human beings, things could not be otherwise. The relevant counterexample would be of a child whose learning began at the formal level and then proceeded to the concrete. While such a case may be conceivable as it does not seem to involve a straightforward logical contradiction, we would at least have to say that it is abnormal. It is part of our understanding of normal human learning that abstract or formal subject matter is harder to acquire than concrete.

If Hamlyn is right, the conclusion that Piaget reached by empirical investigation is reachable by reflection on the implications of concepts we already possess.

It looks as if the same is true about at least some of the factors discovered by SER. It would be an interesting exercise to see how far it is true of other factors. How far can one work out on conceptual grounds that high academic learning depends on such things as shared vision and goals or consistency of purpose? Schools are institutions. How far does the fact that school teaching – as distinct from private tuition, for instance – takes place in an *institution* bring with it the notions that roles have to be coordinated, major inconsistencies have to be ruled out and so on? Consider other instances of the concept of an institution like banks, hospitals, armies. Part of our seeing all these as institutions is that their staff have broadly to be working in the same direction. If vision were not shared at all, if purposes were wholly inconsistent with each other, these would fall apart as institutions. So would schools. We do not need empirical studies to tell us this.

I will not go through all the factors in this way. My main point has been to raise the methodological question whether at least some of the empirical conclusions reached by SER could be reached by non-empirical enquiry.

This is, importantly, not the same as asking whether empirically-derived conclusions are not, after all, a matter of common sense. SER has been charged with this on more than one occasion (see Sammons et al., 1995: 25). The reply has typically been that what seems to be common sense to some people does not always prove to be so, and that we need empirical research to find out whether allegedly common-sense claims actually match reality. Some people, for instance, take it as merely common sense that a stern, punitive classroom regime is best for getting good academic results. But SER evidence undermines this.

It is important to distinguish the claim about logical implications that I have been putting forward from this claim about common sense. I am *not* dealing with beliefs that different people take for granted as obviously true: I readily agree that some of these are empirically unsound. It may seem obvious to some people that working class people tend to be of low intelligence, but there is no good evidence for this belief. The line that I have been pressing examines the logical implications of the concepts used by educational researchers and seeks to show that certain conclusions could not (logically) be otherwise. There is no implication in the concept of successful academic learning that classrooms must be punitive; but there *is*, I am suggesting, an implication that they must be orderly. That is not just someone or other's common-sense belief: it could not normally be otherwise.

The argument in this section has cast doubt on the claim that we need empirical research in order to identify the factors shown to be conducive to effective schools. This is not always true. Sometimes logical analysis can show this – both more swiftly and at a fraction of the cost.

Comparative data on the factors

Let us return to the international aspects of the research. An often-repeated argument used by SE researchers has to do with data from different countries. Reynolds (1989: 20) finds 'impressive' the fact that American research on school effectiveness identifies similar factors to the British research.

But how far does the fact that the same factors turn up again and again in SER in country after country *really* lend weight to the research findings? If I am right, that some factors can be derived from the outcomes by exploring logical implications, this international consistency is precisely what one would expect. What would be surprising would be if the Dutch, Australians, or Americans found that orderly classrooms, careful monitoring of pupil progress or, perhaps, shared vision and goals were *not* associated with high academic achievement.

In so far as SE researchers rely on the consistency of international data as empirical evidence for the view that factor-variables and outcomes are causally related and not merely linked by high correlations (see Mortimore 1995b), their reliance may well be misplaced.

Long-term and short-term goals

I would like to come back now to the earlier points that the notion of 'effectiveness' often stretches beyond means-end considerations towards implications that the ends are good ones; and that the desirability of the ends (outcomes) used in SER may come to be taken as read.

Writing about managerial effectiveness and making use of an argument by Bittner, MacIntyre makes the point that problems arise whether the goals are long-term or short-term.

> Long-term goals cannot be used definitely for calculating (efficiency) because the impact of contingent factors multiplies with time and makes it increasingly difficult to assign a determinate value to the efficiency of a stably controlled segment of action. On the other hand, the use of short-term goals in judging efficiency may be in conflict with the ideal of economy itself. Not only do short-term goals change with time and compete with one another in indeterminate ways, but short-term results are of notoriously deceptive value because they can be easily manipulated to show whatever one wishes them to show (MacIntyre, 1981: 72 – quoting Bittner, 1965: 247).

The relevance of this to school effectiveness should be plain. Education, including school education, has long-term goals. It is about forming young people so that they become adults with such and such desirable characteristics – skills, dispositions, kinds of understanding. Suppose, for instance, one aim is that people come to see themselves as members of a democratic political community, concerned that every member of that community has the wherewithal to lead a flourishing life. (Any other long-term aim would do as well for this purpose.) How would one know whether some schools were more effective than others in achieving this aim? A research programme to determine this would be virtually impossible to devise. Even if one could work out unproblematic testable indices of such a disposition (which would itself need much further refinement of what it was to be taken to mean), so that one could test to what extent products of different schools measured up at ages 20, 30, 40 and so on, one could not get any further unless there were clear differences between schools (an unlikely outcome seeing that there are so many other possible non-school influences on individuals which might account for their having higher or lower scores).

In fact, we simply do not know, and could possibly never know, how effective schools are at cultivating long-term dispositions or other long-term pupil characteristics. SER is limited to short-term 'outcomes'. It seeks to find out which schools are better at producing such things as high literacy or numeracy scores, good GCSE results or low truancy rates.

Why are outcomes like this chosen? If there were evidence that good results on short-term outcomes like these led to good results on long-term goals, SER might justifiably claim to pick out those schools which were better at doing what education is supposed to be about: forming people of a certain sort. But there is no such evidence that I know (and it is hard to see there could be any).

Sammons et al. write:

> Most attention, due to their importance in determining employment and further and higher education chances, tends to focus on measures of schools' academic performance in terms of GCSE or A Level results at the secondary level. On their own, however, such results are not sufficient for proper judgements about schools' performance. Other outcomes such as student attendance, attitudes to school and to learning, behaviour and self-concept are also important. In Britain school effectiveness has often looked at a broad range of educational outcomes to obtain a more comprehensive picture of performance. Nonetheless, the prime importance of academic outcomes must be acknowledged, and it is for this reason that I believe it is essential that a range of useful information about pupil progress is employed in any comparisons of schools. A school which was able to promote social and affective outcomes yet failed in promoting academic progress, could not be classified as truly effective. (Sammons et al., 1995)

In this passage the focus on academic outcomes is justified in terms of their importance in determining employment and further education/higher education chances. This is what gives academic outcomes their 'prime importance'. But why are employment and further education/higher education chances accorded such a priority? There is a good case for claiming that vocational aims should have *some* place in education, but no good case that I know of to give them priority. A totalitarian school system might want high academic achievements in order to stock higher education institutions and certain vocations, but we would not think such achievements desirable in *that* context. Whether or not they are desirable in our own context depends on wider considerations, about the kind of society and the kind of citizen which they are meant to subserve.

The passage also states that other things than academic achievement are important, albeit of less importance – student attendance, attitudes to school and to learning, behaviour and self-concept. Again, no reason why these things are important is provided, although it looks as if they have been included to help meet the charge that education is about many-sided development, not just academic achievement.

Goals and outcomes

An important conceptual distinction emerges here, between goals and outcomes. Take the outcome to do with truancy rates, based on school attendance figures. Having low truancy rates cannot be an *educational goal* of a school. It is not on a par with academic achievement, i.e. as something which teachers aim at and for which the school exists; rather, ensuring it is a necessary condition of academic achievement, in that unless children come to school they cannot produce good academic results.

The question now arises why SER puts together both academic achievements and necessary conditions thereof, like attendance, under the heading of 'outcomes'. Seeing how effective a school – or a commercial firm – is is normally taken to be a matter of seeing how far it achieves certain goals. Disputes may arise, as we have seen, about whether those goals should be short-term or long-term, but at least goal-meeting is the touchstone.

The outcomes used in SER thus seem arbitrary. No good reasons are given for emphasizing academic outcomes. (I do not mean to imply that I think academic goals unimportant. On the contrary. It is the absence of a satisfactory rationale that bothers me.) In addition, the extension of outcomes beyond academic achievements is unexplained. Also, the outcomes are all short-term and no indication is given of how they map on to longer-term objectives.

One feature that all the SE outcomes have, whether academic or non-academic, is that they are measurable. How far has their measurability entered into the reasons why they have been chosen? We do not know, but at least one thing is clear: if this kind of research is to be possible at all, outcomes *have* to be measurable. There is no point in tangling with less hard-edged objectives, however much closer to most people's ideas of educational aims they may be. Measurability is a necessary condition of an outcome, even if it is not sufficient.

This puts a big question mark over the research. Most of the educational aims which parents, teachers and ordinary citizens think important – happiness, personal autonomy, moral goodness, imaginativeness, civic-mindedness or whatever – do not appear to be measurable. We are, therefore, left in ignorance of how effective schools are in bringing about outcomes of a non-measurable sort – precisely the sorts of outcomes that the community at large, as distinct from the educational research community, are often most interested in. This is a central difficulty with the SER programme and cannot be emphasized too much.

(The point about a possible divergence in interests between a research community and the wider community is echoed within the philosophy of education world. Sometimes topics which attract abundant academic attention do so because they are philosophically intriguing, even though they would have little resonance among teachers or parents.)

To come back to the distinction between long- and short-term goals. As MacIntyre pointed out, short-term goals are easily manipulable. The more SE research enters, as it is now doing in a big way, the domain of policy, the more schools will be motivated to make themselves as 'effective' as possible, since financial, prestige and other reasons will press them in this direction. They may make it a high priority to produce the good test scores, GCSE results, low truancy rates or whatever other desiderata the SER may insist on. This may well be at the cost of concentrating on longer-term goals to do with well-roundedness, democratic citizenship, independence of spirit or whatever.

School improvement

Let us turn to the link between SER and SI. As tied to SER, the latter has to do with making less effective schools more effective. Tied in this way, it inherits the former's conceptual drawbacks, not least its limited view of educational goals.

It goes without saying that not all SI schemes have been tied to an SE framework. If misgivings about the latter are well-founded, SI schemes might do better to start from a different point. (For a related thought, see Hargreaves, 1994: 54 – quoted by Gray and Wilcox, 1995: 258.) How might they then proceed?

Above all, they need to be embedded within a thought-structure which links underlying educational aims and values with methods of implementation.

1. If schools are to be improved, they are to be made better. Presumably this is not merely an instrumental matter – of improving the means to a given end, regardless of the value of the end. A school could become better at indoctrinating its pupils in some political ideology, but few would say it was overall a better school for doing so. Making schools better includes making their aims better if these show any deficiencies.

    SI schemes should start, therefore, with ensuring that the aims which, after all, are to power everything else they do are as soundly based as possible. As to what counts as a good set of aims, that is a complex problem which requires among other things philosophical understanding to resolve. This is clearly not the place to begin to go into details, except to say that there is now a wealth of material on which school improvers can draw (e.g. Dearden et al., 1972, Part 1;

Entwistle, 1990: 3–137; O'Hear, 1982; White, 1990; and Wringe, 1988.)

2. Once this broad framework of aims has been clarified as well as it can be, the next stage is to see what follows from these aims about sub-aims which are their necessary conditions. For instance, suppose one takes the aim of preparing children to become self-directing citizens of a liberal democratic society (again, this could be replaced by another example and I also realize that this aim needs clarifying and defending by philosophical argument as outlined in the last paragraph), what does this entail as to dispositions, skills and forms of understanding which pupils brought up under this aegis have to have (O'Hear and White 1991)?

Some of the dispositions or personal qualities have been adumbrated already, but others, too, can be deduced. If people are to lead a self-determined life – unlike, say, the custom-directed life of a tribal community – they have to have:

- a certain moral courage to withstand conformist pressures
- commitment to their self-chosen enterprises and the confidence to think they can succeed in them
- good judgement in deliberation and action when faced with conflicting goals or obligations.

These and other desiderata can be worked out logically once the broader framework is given.

As for some of the kinds of knowledge and understanding that apprentice liberal democrats need, these, too, can be identified fairly easily. If self-determination of one's major goals in life is a defining feature of the liberal-democratic ideal, it follows that one needs some understanding of the various options from among which to choose one's major goals. There is a pretty obvious route here to the familiar educational goal in a society like ours of broadening pupils' horizons, of opening up new possibilities for them in, for instance, the arts, recreational activities, careers, lifestyles and intellectual pursuits such as the pursuit of mathematics or science for its own sake. Similarly, becoming a liberal-democratic citizen requires some understanding of the society of which one is to become a citizen – its geography and history, its sociological and economic structure, the scientific-technological basis of the latter, its political arrangements, etc. Literacy and numeracy skills are seen to be obvious desiderata round about this point.

The last paragraph has brought in academic objectives, some of whose short-term versions are prominent in SER. It shows that if the civic aims suggested are important, then academic ones must be, too. Some sort of rationale is, in this way, provided for the latter. This, in embryo, might help to meet the problem we met earlier about the paucity of reasons that SE researchers have given for stressing academic aims. The rationale needs to be filled out in all sorts of ways, of course, as it is too brief and crude.

3.   Philosophical reflection can take one only so far in identifying aims and sub-aims. After a certain point, one has to call on more specific forms of expertise. The historian's, for instance, in helping one to work out with which features of the history of their own society pupils need indispensably to be acquainted, assuming that this kind of historical understanding has been shown in general to be desirable.

So far 1. to 3. have shown us a route to determining the *content* of education, including in this its aims. SI schemes need to start here. Of course, in practice this is not something that can be left to a single school or even to a group of schools within a school improvement project. The content of school education is, at least in its larger framework, decided outside the school, usually, as in England and Wales, at the national political level. This should encourage us to take a broad view of the scope of school improvement schemes, including within it attempts at the highest political levels to work out acceptable National Curriculum objectives. More local or small-scale

SI projects, focusing, as most do, on processes rather than content, still need to bear in mind the primacy of content. This means that they cannot accept unquestioningly the National Curriculum framework in which they may be working. Part of any school improvement scheme must be support for reflection on the adequacy of such a framework and for attempts to make it more soundly based.

4. Once content has been determined, the spotlight falls on the *procedures* by which this content is taught and learnt. As should be evident from the previous section on school effectiveness, to some extent procedures can be derived by reflection on logical implications. We come back to such things as orderly classrooms, structured lessons and shared goals among the staff.

5. As with content, philosophical thinking can take one only so far. At a more specific level we have to rely on specialist expertise, in this case the teacher as organizer of learning, both within the classroom and at whole-school level. Good teachers have plenty of experience of trying this approach and that approach and their practical wisdom is sharable with others. SI studies have been especially strong in reviewing and communicating this expertise.

SI schemes need to be set within the 1.–5. thought-framework. They must also take into account features of particular schools. Given the 1. to 5. framework, they are in a position to see how far a school measures up to it and where there are any shortfalls, either in content or in procedures. It will often be important to explain why these shortfalls have occurred so that ways of overcoming them can be worked out. The methodology of explanation is that of the historian rather than of the scientist. It will require, for instance, coming to see how it is that a school is generally lax on discipline, tracing back the causes of the present situation to earlier policies, staff appointments and so on.

Given all this, the practical work can then start, of devising means to overcome whatever obstacles lie in the way of the school's progress. Thinking thus proceeds in two directions – from underlying values through to specifics and from the actual situation a school is in towards a better situation. Both are patterns of practical rather than theoretical reasoning, in that they aim primarily at realizing the good rather than at discovering truths. At the same time, both draw on theoretical reasoning (e.g. about what has caused a school's lax discipline) as a part of attaining their practical aims.

Although I have presented the two patterns of practical thinking along logical lines, suggesting that the first comes before the second and that the first proceeds from 1. through to 5. and then into school-related specifics, in practice this logical order need not be matched by a temporal order of proceeding. A school's disciplinary arrangements might be knocked into better shape while its curriculum is left as it is. More generally, there can be all sorts of improvements to a school's procedures (or to 'process') independently of attention to content. There is nothing necessarily wrong about this, of course, but it does need to be re-emphasized that school improvement depends on soundly based content, that is, it must take 1. to 3. seriously. Otherwise it may find itself devising better and better ways of bringing about inadequate or downright bad ends.

Methodological issues

I have suggested that school improvement is best seen as a form of practical reasoning and action in accordance with it. This encompasses instrumental reasoning about what means to adopt to reach certain ends, but is not exhausted by it, since not only does it require reflection on ends themselves, but in addition ends can put constraints on means, raising doubts about those with which they seem to be incompatible. Suppose, for instance, that from a purely instrumental point of view, classroom discipline could be best achieved in a particular school by a regime of terror such as is described in James Joyce's celebrated account of the use of the 'pandybat' in *A Portrait of the Artist as a Young Man* (1960: 48–51). If the school aimed among other things at preparation for democratic citizenship, such draconianism might well get in the way of this.

This emphasis on thinking about ends as w
this more specific context, what Aristotle wrote
about what is involved in living a flourishing hu
distinction between the practically wise person
merely clever or intelligent: whereas the latter is
thinking regardless of the value of the end, the fo⌐   ⌐rizons are
wider, embracing thought about ends with the aim of locating those most
soundly based.

The methodology of SER, to come back to this, is very different. The
research literature gives minimal evidence of reflection on ends. There
is some; but it does not extend very far. Stoll and Mortimore write:

> Ultimately, school effectiveness research searches for appropriate
> and reliable ways to measure school quality. The concept of
> 'effectiveness' forces choices to be made among competing values.
> While some people choose a narrow approach with a basic skills
> emphasis, others perceive schools' aims to be more diverse.
>
> (Stoll and Mortimore, 1995: 1)

As for the last statement, we have already seen how some SER goes
beyond academic attainments into things like attitudes to school, truancy
and self-concept. We have seen, too, how we are left with arbitrary items
which lack connection with longer-term aims. And what does it mean to
say that the concept of 'effectiveness' forces choices among competing
values? I think what the authors must have had in mind is that to get
effectiveness research going at all, one must start with outcomes with
which the research can deal, in effect measurable outcomes. But there
are different sorts of measurable outcomes, e.g. academic and non-
academic, as we have just seen. What the SE researcher has to do is
choose among them. The implication seems to be that choice is the only
course of action possible: it is, as the passage states, 'forced' upon one.
Other alternatives, e.g. reflection on ends to see whether those proposed
are rationally supportable, seem to be ruled out.

SE researchers see themselves as following a *scientific* paradigm, in
that they are posing questions which can only be answered by empirical

...stigation coupled with mathematical analysis, which, unlike empirical historical research, aims at discovering generalizations, applicable across a range of cases. The empirical generalizations which it claims to have found are about factors conducive to effectiveness. About these I have already claimed that, far from being empirical discoveries, some at least are deducible largely by reflection on logical implications. This last claim casts doubt on how far a scientific paradigm can take one in this kind of research.

The scientific perspective informing SE/SI research is underlined in Mortimore's comment that:

> Although school effectiveness and school improvement work has been led, in general, by empirical investigations, there has been an increasing preoccupation with the need for the development of an underpinning theory. This lack of a sufficiently specific theory has been compensated for, in part, by the use of a range of other theories culled from child development, management science and the sociological, psychological and institutional fields. Recently, the literature on change has also been drawn upon. The need for an integrated theory, however, remains.
>
> (Mortimore, 1995a)

Why should SE/SI research require an underpinning theory? What, indeed, is meant by 'theory' in this context? It is plainly not a theory in the sense of a hypothesis awaiting confirmation or disconfirmation, like a historian's theory about the causes of the collapse of the Soviet Empire. Could it be a theory in the sense of a higher-order explanatory system integrating lower-order explanations of phenomena by laws – like molecular theory, for instance, which accounts for the operations of the Gas Laws? If so, it would seem to be fruitless to look for a theory underpinning SE/SI research, since, as we have seen, at the lower order there seem to be no laws for a theory to explain.

SE/SI research is pulled in two opposite methodological directions – Galilean and Aristotelian, towards science and towards practical reasoning. SER would seem to belong to the former paradigm, but whether scientific investigation makes sense in this context is open to doubt. SI work faces the same objection in so far as it is tied to school effectiveness research. But much of the literature of SI falls within the other paradigm: it deals with obstacles that schools must overcome and ways of making things better. As I argued earlier, SI work could well broaden its horizons within this paradigm to embrace the more philosophical aspects of content-determination as well as – what it has tended to focus on – procedures.

I hope that this critical discussion of SE/SI research is helpful not only for whatever light it may shed on the research itself, but also as an example of how philosophical understanding and approaches can be applied to empirical educational research. There is much more to be said about what it can contribute than I have had space for here. Indeed, if I am right in arguing that SE/SI researchers would benefit by reflection on more fundamental and more long-term educational aims, there is ample room in the future for closer collaboration with philosophers of education.

I look forward to further developments on that front in my own institution. As will be clear from the following Note, it was just such a coming-together which led to this present paper. One of the great pleasures – and privileges – of working at the Institute of Education lies in the opportunities which its size and many-sidedness provide for intellectually stimulating interdisciplinary debate. I look forward to continuing this particular discussion with my more local colleagues as well as with other scholars.

Note

This paper was triggered by a seminar on philosophical aspects of SER at the Institute of Education University of London in autumn 1995 between staff and students of the Philosophy of Education Research Seminar and members of the International School Effectiveness and Improvement Centre (ISEIC). Hence the orientation of the references partly towards work emanating from this Centre. I am most grateful for critical comments on earlier drafts by Michael Barber, Michael Fielding, Harvey Goldstein, John Gray, Abby Riddell, Pam Sammons, David Scott,

Louise Stoll, Sally Thomas, Patricia White, Chris Winch. I am especially indebted to Peter Mortimore, both for the time he took out of his tightly-packed schedule to provide me with very full and helpful comments and also for the further reading material which he sent me.

I take full responsibility for the ideas in this final draft, knowing that many of the commentators just mentioned will not agree with them.

4 Accountability, controversy and school effectiveness research

Christopher Winch

Introduction

I want to start with an apparently uncontroversial idea that often arouses irritation amongst those who work in public sector services, namely that they should be accountable to those who provide the resources to operate them. The basis for the 'should' in the previous sentence is the idea of reciprocal obligation which is fundamental to the idea of trust. This obligation may be obscured by the existence of deferential relationships between lay and professional people, but in a society where deference towards professionals has for long been declining, that relationship of obligation has emerged more clearly into the light.[1] The key question for education is: how can this relationship best be satisfied in a way that both provides accurate information and is fair to those from whom an account is being asked?

There are two distinct but related aspects of accountability: constitutive and qualitative. Constitutive accountability is concerned with whether or not goods or services that should be provided actually are provided and to what level. Qualitative accountability is concerned with seeking ways in which what is provided can be provided in a better form.[2] It is not possible to provide qualitative accountability without some form of constitutive accountability, but the provision of the latter does not entail the provision of the former. The OFSTED school inspection regime cannot really provide for qualitative accountability as it has no mechanism for school improvement other than the provision of a school action plan. The inspectors exist to inspect, not to advise on improvement.

In so far as schools feel impelled to improve after or before inspection, OFSTED provides for a degree of indirect qualitative accountability. At first glance, the publication of school results is an example of constitutive accountability, but if the publication of results in itself leads schools to improve their performance, then there is a case for saying that it provides for a degree of qualitative accountability as well. School effectiveness research (SER) is concerned with the former through an assessment of the rate of progress in academic achievement that pupils make in their schools. It is also concerned with the qualitative aspect of accountability through the identification of features of effective schooling. School improvement research (SIR) is concerned with helping schools to put into effect features that lead to effective schooling and builds on school effectiveness research in order to do so.

Given the availability of performance results and inspection, what can SER offer that makes it a useful and distinctive way of ensuring constitutive accountability? The answer its protagonists give is that it provides a method of identifying the effect that schooling has on pupils' educational achievement, rather than the effects of social class, sex or home background, for example. It thus provides more accurate information than other methods, but it also provides more equitable information because like is compared with like.

How it works

The basic idea of value-added measures is to provide an assessment of progress over a period of education, as opposed to an assessment of achievement at a particular point in time. Value-added measures are, then, logically dependent on measures of achievement because they measure the difference between two measures of achievement, the difference being the main component of the measure of added value. Institutions can then be compared with each other in terms of added value by comparing the amount of progress made between assessment points.

The measures of achievement used to obtain the data usually take one of two forms: first the use of public examination or test results taken at different times; second, some form of tailor-made test designed or adapted for the specific purpose of carrying out a value-added measure. The first type of instrument is most suitable in a system where there is uniform testing at different stages of education which allow for comparisons, within schools, of achievement at different stages. Such a system will become possible in the UK as the assessment associated with the National Curriculum becomes fully established and consistent in its operation. It has been used, for example, by Fitz-Gibbon in her analysis of the value added by sixth form studies. The second approach is commonly adopted by researchers looking at added value in contexts where the requisite testing instruments are not already in place as part of an assessment system. Studies which have adopted this approach include Mortimore et al. (1988) in London junior schools and Tizard et al. (1988), which looked at Inner London infant schools. These studies employed a combination of tests either in use or developed specifically for the purpose of obtaining measures of prior and subsequent achievement. Mortimore et al. used a variety of measures, including a standardized reading test and a creative writing exercise, in order to obtain measures of achievement. In addition, various measures were taken of non-cognitive development, using such instruments as the 'Child at School' questionnaire schedule, which classteachers had to complete (Mortimore et al, 1988:102). A similar approach was used by the study of Tizard et al. into progress in London infant schools.

Fitz-Gibbon argues that value-added measures can be made more meaningful by controlling for other factors that may affect educational achievement such as home background, ability or prior achievement. In this way, those factors for which the school is not responsible, but which may, nevertheless, have an effect on achievement are taken into account. The statistical technique known as multilevel modelling is usually used to provide this sort of analysis.[3] In the Mortimore et al. and Tizard et al. studies, it was then possible to compute progress in various areas, both cognitive (connected with the curriculum) and non-cognitive (connected with behaviour and attitudes) between different assessment points. As with the Fitz-Gibbon study, residuals (the differences between initial and final achievement) were computed, taking into account relevant background factors affecting achievement, for which the schools were not responsible, using multilevel modelling.

If we adopt the principle that people should only be accountable for those acts for which they are responsible or for those factors which it is within their power to influence, then we must be cautious in making judgements about educational institutions when it is not entirely clear what is and what is not within their influence and to what extent. This implies that any judgement about whether a school is doing a good or a bad job needs to be based on a distinction between those aspects of adding value that the school can influence and those it cannot. It should be possible, for example, for a school to have control over pedagogy, it is far less clear that it can control for the background of its pupils or, more crucially, the effects that the pupils' backgrounds may have on their learning and on the way in which they can be taught.

All such measurements are subject to both measurement and statistical error and results can only be interpreted within confidence intervals which overlap considerably. The most that one can say with any degree of confidence about these measures is that they appear to identify the following three groups of schools.

1. A majority whose performances are not at the extremes of either effectiveness or ineffectiveness and are broadly comparable with each other.
2. A group whose effectiveness is measurably greater than the first group.
3. A group whose effectiveness is measurably less than the first group.

(See Woodhouse and Goldstein, 1988: 301–20.)

There is, however, a more disturbing possibility, namely that even this general result might be compromised by a further error factor which cannot be compensated for within the existing methodology, without stretching the range of measurement error to such an extent that there can be no meaningful value-added comparisons between schools. The problem arises when pupil-level data is used as the basis for calculating residuals (the measure of the difference between the two performances). There are good reasons for doing this as data aggregated at higher levels is subject to statistical error. However, since some pupils move from school to school between the measurement periods, their performance cannot be used to calculate residuals. When significant numbers of pupils are involved, it will be very difficult, if not impossible, to calculate a residual for the school.

If residuals are no longer to be the basis for calculating school effectiveness, then how could it be assessed? One answer would be to look at the practices in classrooms that make for effective learning. Smaller-scale studies could measure incremental gains in learning within a short enough timescale for losses from pupil movement not to compromise before-after measures. But, in focusing on practice, SER will need to be very clear about where it stands in the hotly contested debate about 'good practice'. Carr has criticized Alexander for seeing the question about whether or not practice is good as a purely technical matter not informed by values (Alexander, 1992; and Carr, 1994). I think that it can be argued that Alexander is not open to this accusation but, like Carr himself, he does not see, or at least does not show that he is aware, that the adoption of values in the classroom is a highly political matter, rather than a purely ethical one, and involves the aims for which education is undertaken.[4] It follows that if classroom practice is to be assessed in a way that takes account of its value dimension, an articulation of the aims against which it is to be assessed is unavoidable. At the very least, judgements about practice can only be made relative to certain aims. These aims need to be made explicit if the judgements are to be properly understood. This is the kind of debate that school effectiveness researchers have tended to fight shy of, even though it is central to their concerns. However, it will be argued in the next section that even if the methodological problems mentioned earlier are surmountable, an engagement with questions concerning the aims of education cannot long be delayed if such research is to continue in fruitful ways.[5]

One final point about the methodological aspects of SER and its political implications needs to be dealt with. SER has, quite properly, been fully aware of, and has constantly drawn attention to, the problem of inferential hazard and the need for caution in interpreting residuals. The reason that researchers have adopted such a cautious approach has been an acute awareness that the credibility of the whole enterprise rests on its ability to make judgements that really are backed up by the available evidence. But the very scrupulousness of SER is bound to have implications for other, less careful, ways of securing educational accountability. If such attention to validity, reliability and making judgements subject to measurement and statistical error is right for SER, why is it not also a requirement for, say, OFSTED, whose work is on a far larger scale and whose judgements are of far greater consequence? Given the amounts of public money spent on OFSTED to secure school accountability, the accountability of OFSTED itself should come under some scrutiny. SER, with its experience of the dangers inherent in making judgements about schools, would be well placed to do this and, arguably has a duty to do so. There is no evidence whatsoever that OFSTED has exercised anything like the methodological care in making judgements, nor the caution in pronouncing those judgements that SER has been careful to exercise. A consequence of the difficulties of SER is that the credibility of OFSTED is under considerable doubt. Like SER, OFSTED has kept away from a view of what constitutes good classroom practice by not commenting on the aims against which it is assessing schools and by defining good teaching and learning in such a way as be offering a constitutive defininition of what constitutes teaching and learning, rather than a qualitative one (OFSTED, 1994). Both SER and OFSTED have avoided controversial definitions of good practice by using 'commonsensical' (see 'School effectiveness research and qualitative accountability' below) definitions of what these are. But this is not an illuminating way of saying anything useful about these issues; it is rather a temporary expedient for avoiding controversy.

Should SER be disseminated to the public?

SER is, then, a highly technical discipline which relies on a number of assumptions that are themselves contestable within the research paradigm in which it arises. The accurate interpretation of results is a matter which requires expertise in statistics and is not, therefore, readily intelligible to the general public. This poses a problem for the proponents of SER, for, if information about value-added is released into the public domain, then there is a danger that it will be misleading. If this is a danger for value-added data then *a fortiori* by the arguments of the previous section it is for OFSTED inspection data as well. On the other hand, if it is not released then what information is the public entitled to in relation to school performance? The premise of SER is that one-shot test results are misleading without both a measure of progress and an interpretative context. So they should not be released either, by the same argument. But then, the public is not entitled to any information about the performance of schools. Constitutive accountability seems to be under threat. But this is an absurd position; it may well be the case that the results of SER are a form of esoteric scientific knowledge and this consideration may lead one to think that they are a better tool for policy analysis and formation than they are for public accountability purposes. The most that they will be able to tell the public with any degree of confidence is that a school is performing above, below or at the norm. In due course, as time-series data becomes available they will also provide a picture of how the norm changes over time.

But it does not follow from these considerations that no information should be given to the public concerning the aggregate results of tests and exams. It is true that one-shot results cannot provide information about progress or about context and it is also true that they are subject to a degree of random fluctuation year by year (this can, however, be corrected by the use of rolling three-year averages). But it does not follow that they provide no information of any use to parents, the general public or the schools. Pupils, parents, employers and schools are primarily interested in the achievement of pupils at school, rather than their progress; it is achievement at various key points that disclose knowledge, ability and understanding. Parents will, in particular, wish to know what the likely results are going to be of sending their child to a school with a characteristic pattern of achievement. They can infer, with reasonable safety, certain things about a school from the pattern of achievement. For example, they will be able to infer that a school which achieves 0 per cent of grades A–C at GCSE over a three-year period is unlikely to have very high expectations of the pupils and that there is unlikely to be a strongly developed interest in academic achievement amongst the pupils themselves. They will also be able to infer, with reasonable safety, that it is less likely that their own child will do as well as he might in such a school than if he goes to a school where the comparable proportion is 40 per cent. None of these inferences have the certainty of deduction, few of the inferences we make in daily life do, but this does not diminish their utility. These arguments apply to a certain extent to value-added data. It can be inferred, with reasonable safety, that a pupil attending a school where progress is below the norm is less likely to achieve well than if he or she were to attend a school where progress is at or above the norm for progress. If this information about schools (which could be coded into three categories), is put together with information about results at critical assessment points, then parents and the public will be able to make reasonable, if rather general, inductive inferences about the future achievement of pupils at particular schools.

But there are other arguments for publishing aggregate scores and rudimentary measures of pupil progress. It is necessary, when considering the introduction of a measure, to consider not only the disadvantages of doing so, but also the disadvantages of not doing so. Here there is a strong case for saying that failure to publish information about achievement will lead to a collapse of confidence in public schooling. Failure to publish results suggests that there is something to hide. Furthermore, it also means that no major instrument of constitutive accountability is available, apart from the flawed judgements of OFSTED. The disillusion with education that is likely to set in if such a policy were adopted would threaten the rationale for accreditation, which forms one of the ways in which a public education system is accepted by broader interests in society. For an argument along these lines, see an article by Tooley where it is proposed that conventional assessment can be replaced with universal IQ testing at around the age of ten (Tooley, 1995).

Some will object that the whole enterprise of focusing on exam results and tests is a travesty of educational aims. Those who believe that schools are essentially concerned with moral development or with personal liberation will protest that the emphasis on tests, results and academic progress is fundamentally anti-educational. It is difficult to have sympathy with such a view from the perspective of a publicly accountable education service. There is no doubt that some people may wish to educate their children with either moral development or personal liberation as a major or even an exclusive aim. Neither is there much doubt that few parents would be happy with schooling that paid little or no attention to moral development or the promotion of at least a certain degree of autonomy. But neither is there the slightest reason to suppose that there is a strong current of opinion that does not regard achievement of knowledge, skill and understanding in academic and practical subjects as among the most important aims that a public education system ought to pursue. The point here relates to accountability once again. If, either explicitly or implicitly, resources are provided for public education on the understanding that a major commitment be made to the measurable achievement of knowledge, skill and understanding in academic and practical subjects, those who are in receipt of public monies on that understanding are under a moral commitment to measurably reach such goals. This should be clear enough, not least to those who think that the development of moral virtues is one of the major tasks of public education.

So far we have established that both one-shot results and, possibly, an elementary form of value-added data have a good claim to serve as instruments of constitutive accountability. It is now time to turn to the relationship between SER and qualitative accountability.

School effectiveness research and qualitative accountability

Associated with measures of effectiveness, SER has claimed to identify factors associated with effective schools. These include:

- collegiate decision-making
- strong leadership
- high expectations of pupils
- an orderly classroom environment
- concentration on one curriculum area at a time

- purposeful teaching
- attention to assessment (Mortimore et al., 1988, Chapter 11; and Mortimore, 1995: 11).

It seems plausible to suggest that the identification of these factors of effective schooling can be followed by their implementation in schools that do not currently have these features, or which have them imperfectly. Those who are not involved professionally in education, and many who are, will find them unsurprising. The only surprise might lie in finding that not all schools share such features, since it is so obvious that they are likely to lead to effective learning. In this respect, SER does not seem to have told us very much that was not already common sense, or even *a priori* knowledge.

However, as in most areas of education, matters are not quite as simple as this. As Gramsci argued, there is more than just one version of common sense (Gramsci, 1971: 323–3 and 419–25). On the Gramscian view, common sense is a theoretically more or less well-developed world view as it is manifested in everyday life. Gramsci was particularly interested in the different common-sense views of the world manifested in the lives of the members of different social classes, but his analysis has some plausibility in relation to the world views of the lay public on the one hand and professional groups on the other. In particular, it can be argued that certain important sections of the education profession, particularly those involved in training, inspection and academic research, have developed a world view which is expressive of different common sense from that of the lay public (see Selleck, 1972). This world view, based on the moral psychology set out in Rousseau's *Emile* and in the work of subsequent progressive educational writers such as Dewey, stresses the harmful effects of the imposition of authority on children and suggests personal liberation as the primary goal of education.[6]

These views have certain implications for classroom practice. It is far from obvious that classrooms should be orderly in the sense that they are controlled by an authoritative teacher; since the aim of the progressive project is personal liberation, the imposition of a curriculum by knowledgeable and enthusiastic teachers could be seen as inimical to that development. Likewise, the imposition of a set of high academic expectations that arc not consonant with the wishes of the child might be seen as a harmfully authoritarian approach, as would the imposition of a single curriculum subject at a single time in a classroom when some pupils might wish to follow different patterns of activity. Assessment too, should be related to the child's aims rather than those of the teacher (Carr, 1995: 55).

Viewed in this way, although some might see SER as a rather expensive and highly technical way of stating the obvious, others might see it as the covert imposition of a reactionary alternative common sense about education in the guise of esoteric scientific knowledge (see Ball (ed.), 1990). The picture that now emerges of SER is a highly political one: it appears to be an internal critique from within the education service, of the most cherished assumptions of some of those who work within that service. Instead of discovering exciting and new scientifically validated knowledge concerning what makes schools effective, it may be seen as suggesting a pattern for ensuring qualitative accountability which is designed to overturn a number of cherished professional assumptions about educational aims and practice.

If SER is actually in the business of reintroducing a new common sense (an old one in non-educational contexts) into the education service and doing so in a covert way, then the seemingly bland and apparently uncontroversial nature of its findings will become more intelligible. New and potentially unpalatable ideas can be introduced into educational thinking in a way that renders them apparently less threatening. For example, old common sense is presented as esoteric scientific knowledge: the idea of added value appears to be both child and school centred. It is the child's progress that is the central focus of concern and it is the work of the school and its teachers, often in unfavourable circumstances, that become the focus of scrutiny and, possibly, favourable comment. The concern helps to deflect what is seen as a crude, neo-liberal demand for accountability through the publication of uninterpreted league tables. Really controversial hypotheses that could not readily be seen simply as a part of an alternative common-sense view of the world are avoided. These include segregation by ability, sex or interest – all of which have been thought by some to contribute to effective schooling and the raising of standards, but all of which are thought to contradict egalitarian aims of education.

Leading SE researchers have spoken of the need to develop more general principles or even a theory of SE (e.g. Mortimore, 1995: 16–19). By this they mean the development of some general principles for the identification and promotion of school effectiveness. If the argument just given is correct, all that they have so far achieved is the partial reinstatement of an older, non-professional common-sense view of teaching and learning. This observation to some extent defines the real nature of the task that confronts SER in the development of theory. The kind of theory that needs to be developed is a clearer articulation of educational aims as these are seen by SE researchers, rather than the development of generalizations on the basis of empirical findings. This kind of theory building is likely to be controversial, but, in the interests of openness and the prevention of misunderstanding it should now be carried out. There has, in any event, been very little clear and frank debate about what the appropriate mix of educational aims for the British education system should be, and this has resulted in a great deal of vagueness and confusion. SE researchers could make a big contribution to this debate by stating their position.[7]

Having done this they would then be in a position to consider some of the more interesting and controversial questions that relate to SE. Aims such as academic achievement, social cohesion, the development of virtuous citizens and egalitarianism are not necessarily in conflict with each other, but they are often in competetition. Whenever they cannot be pursued jointly on the curriculum or in the same school, they must be pursued separately. If they are pursued separately, they will need a distinct amount of time or they will consume extra resources in order to do so. Since a limited amount of time and resources are available and since there are opportunity costs attached to choosing any alternative, decisions on what mix of aims to go for and what weighting to attach to each, become decisions which involve balancing gains and losses.[8] There are many people who are broadly in agreement about the range of aims that an educational system ought to pursue, but who, nevertheless, disagree about the relative weighting of those aims. They would be very interested to see what were the various costs and benefits of weighting aims in different ways to use in evidence in any debate about the weighting of aims. It may be that a trade-off between benefits and costs that was thought to exist does not in fact exist, or it may be found that a correlation that was thought to exist does not, in fact, do so. In these circumstances, the proper approach will be investigation of what happens under different conditions.

It is worth taking a few examples to see the kind of questions that might be asked and answered.

1. The desirability or otherwise of streaming in relation to both to academic achievement and to pupil disaffection.[9]
2. The relationship between single sex schooling and academic achievement.
3. Providing genuine diversity in the secondary curriculum and its possible effect on pupil disaffection, together with evaluation of a wider range of academic-related and practical outcomes in the upper years of the secondary school.
4. The consequences of the provision of preschooling on subsequent academic and non-academic outcomes.
5. An examination of the relationship between gaining maximum academic achievement for particular individuals and maximizing aggregate levels of academic achievement.
6. An assessment of the role that inspection can play in assessing effectiveness.

These are all issues that deserve consideration because of the historical and current lack of clarity about aims within the English and Welsh education systems. Research into these areas might allow those interested in the effectiveness of our education system to make considered judgements concerning the balance between educational achievement and various social goals, between different configurations of what is to count as educational achievement and the use of highly intrusive accountability procedures in assessing effectiveness. These are all highly political issues in the sense that they concern the different points of view different groups in society may have concerning education, its aims and the values that it expresses. However, this is hardly a reason for ignoring them.

Mortimore suggests the following as worthy topics in the search for school improvement:

1.　the effectiveness of different models of intervention
2.　different strategies of action (focusing on both the classroom and on other dimensions such as the governing body and management arrangements)
3.　different ways of ensuring the optimum match of intervention strategy to the context and circumstances of the individual school (Mortimore, 1995: 20).

Of these, 1. is a vast topic but does not, of itself, sound particularly controversial. However, 6. on my list is subsumed in Mortimore's 1., and is very much concerned with ensuring accountability given the vast hidden and overt costs of the OFSTED regime and would be highly controversial but potentially very illuminating. 2. is vague and lacks explicitness. What are the particular issues that inform this concern? Are they about pedagogy? Or about pedagogy in particular subject areas? What is the nature of the concern with the relationship between management and classroom practice? 3. is more specific but involves the putting into effect of the findings already noted into particular circumstances, when one of the key issues in the whole debate about SE is the extent to which these are findings which are genuinely informative.

There is, then, a continuing suggestion that SER has to tread very carefully in relation to issues that are politically sensitive. This may be the safest way forward in a world of insecure funding and uncertainty about credibility and popularity. However, by not taking any risks, the whole movement is exposed to the danger of not providing interesting answers to questions that its external audiences may be interested in on the one hand, and failing to lull the suspicions of its critics within the world of education on the other. This would be a pity, as the question of how we should prioritize and configure educational aims is one of the most pressing ones facing British education today and is one in which those working in SER have the capacity to provide the evidence to help determine the answers.

Conclusion

SER has to engage in the debate about the nature of the aims of schooling if it is to be properly recognized for what it is and if it is to be more frank about the kind of political impact that it seeks to make. It needs, in particular, to define its position in relation to the following questions.

1. What importance should the place of (a) academic and (b) vocational or practical qualifications have in the specification of educational aims?

2. How important are the achievement of moral aims such as the development of virtuous citizens, egalitarianism or the achievement of strong autonomy in relations to the achievement of 1.?

However, although this will make SER more controversial, it will also have the merit of allowing researchers to look at some of the more interesting issues that have not so far been tackled. There is a sense in which SER is now at a crossroads and decisions have to be taken about how it is to develop further if the public and the education service are to continue to take it seriously. My suggestion is that it is now at a stage at which theoretical work is seriously overdue, but not, perhaps in quite the way that Mortimore has suggested. There can as yet be no general theory of what makes schools effective because no such theory could make sense without an idea of what mix of aims the public education system should adopt. So far, SER has adopted a low-level approach to this question, relying on the implicit common sense of the general public, who see academic achievement as the main criterion of effective schooling. But the critics within the education system, particularly in the academic world, are already wary and, however misconceived their objections might be, they will need to be taken on if SER is to establish itself as a serious intellectual enterprise concerned with altering the direction and performance of much of our education system. It cannot continue developing esoteric technical expertise and ignoring wider political and philosophical issues about the nature and future direction of the education service.

Notes

1 But see the discussion in Mill, 1910: 161, where the idea that the autonomy of teachers should be interfered with, even though they are in receipt of state finance, is dismissed as prejudicial to freedom of opinion and speech. Most modern democracies now accept that ensuring the accountability of their education systems is part of their duties and they adopt various strategies to achieve those ends. (See HMSO, 1995.)

2 Sometimes, accountability is taken to refer to the first requirement only, but the two are not separate in that way. Not only is one obliged to spend resources in the area agreed, but one is obliged to spend them in the best possible way. For a more limited view of accountability, see St. John-Brooks, 1995.

3 See Goldstein (1987, Chapter 2). An illustration of the equations used in such an analysis can be found in Tizard et al. (1988, Appendix 3).

4 That is, it involves negotiation about the extent to which differing ethical values can be implemented in the public sphere (see Winch, 1996, Chapter 6).

5 There are, in any case, disagreements amongst SER researchers about the kinds of model that are most appropriate to the assessment of school effectiveness. See the defence of data envelopment analysis by Mayston and Jesson (1988: 321–40) and the reply in Woodhouse and Goldstein (1988).

6 For the idea that teachers develop different common-sense views of the world in the Gramscian sense, see Carr (1995).

7 It is noteworthy that even one of the frankest and most outspoken of evaluation researchers, Alexander, has not clearly articulated his views on this question, even though he is on record as recognizing the importance of values in the determination of 'good educational practice' (1992).

8 An alternative approach to SE evaluation, data envelopment analysis, although it does not attempt to quantify trade-offs between aims, does attempt to show how there can be relative gains and losses in relation to expenditure and achievement.

9 It is curious that contemporary SER has not commented on this issue even though Mortimore et al. include as a reference one of the major studies (that of Barker-Lunn, 1970). In fact, there is quite a literature on this topic dating from the 1960s at least. See, for example, Acland (1972) and Barker-Lunn (1970).

5 Key characteristics of effective schools: a review of school effectiveness research

Pam Sammons
Josh Hillman
Peter Mortimore

Introduction

In 1994 the Office for Standards in Education (OFSTED) commissioned the International School Effectiveness and Improvement Centre (ISEIC) to conduct a review of school effectiveness research summarizing current knowledge about the factors identified in the literature as important in gaining a better understanding of effectiveness. The aim was to provide 'an analysis of the key determinants of school effectiveness in secondary and primary schools'.

Scheerens (1992) has identified the following five areas of research relevant to school effectiveness.

1. Research into equality of opportunity and the significance of the school in this (e.g. Coleman et al., 1966; and Jencks et al., 1972).

2. Economic studies of education production functions (e.g. Hanushek, 1979 and 1986).

3. The evaluation of compensatory programmes (e.g. Stebbins et al., 1977; and reviews by Purkey and Smith, 1983; and Van der Grift, 1987).

4. Studies of effective schools and the evaluation of school improvement programmes. (For studies of effective schools, see

Brookover et al., 1979; Rutter et al., 1979; and Mortimore et al., 1988a. For the evaluation of improvement programmes, see the review by Miles et al., 1983.)

5. Studies of the effectiveness of teachers and teaching methods (see reviews by Walberg, 1984; Stallings, 1985; Doyle, 1985; and Brophy and Good, 1986).

Although our primary focus is on the school effectiveness tradition, in conducting our review we have examined research in the related field of teacher effectiveness. Where appropriate, however, we also refer to work in the other three areas identified by Scheerens. It is important to take account of the relationships between school factors (e.g. policies, leadership and culture) and classroom processes, because in some institutions the former may provide a more supportive environment for teaching and learning than others (Purkey and Smith, 1983; Mortimore et al., 1988a; Fullan and Hargreaves, 1992; Scheerens, 1992; Reynolds et al., 1994; and Stoll and Fink, 1994). Where appropriate, we refer to the results of previous reviews of literature in these fields (e.g. Purkey and Smith, 1983; Ralph and Fennessey, 1983; Rutter, 1983; Doyle, 1986; Walberg, 1986; Fraser et al., 1987; Rosenshine, 1987; Reid et al., 1987; Levine and Lezotte, 1990; North West Regional Educational Laboratory, 1990; Reynolds and Cuttance, 1992; Scheerens, 1992; Reynolds et al., 1994; and Tabberer, 1994). We draw attention to some of the limitations of existing school effectiveness research, particularly the weak theoretical basis (Scheerens, 1992; Reynolds and Cuttance, 1992; Creemers, 1994; and Hopkins, 1994), and the fact that the number of empirical studies which focus directly on the characteristics of effective schools is exceeded by the number of reviews of the area.

We note the need for caution in interpreting findings concerning 'key determinants' of effectiveness based on evidence much of which, in the early research, is derived from studies of the characteristics of small numbers of outlier schools (selected as either highly effective or highly ineffective). The dangers of interpreting correlations as evidence of causal mechanisms are also highlighted. For example, reciprocal relationships may well be important, as may intermediate causal relationships. Thus, high expectations may enhance student achievement, which in turn promotes high expectations for succeeding age groups. Improved achievement may benefit behavioural outcomes which in turn foster later achievement. Conversely, lower expectations may become self-fulfilling, poor attendance and poor behaviour may lead to later academic under-achievement which exacerbates behavioural and attendance problems and so on. Despite these caveats, however, we conclude that such a review has value in synthesizing current school effectiveness findings in an accessible format and providing an analysis of key factors likely to be of relevance to practitioners and policy-makers concerned with school improvement and enhancing quality in education.

Background

The major impetus for development of North American and UK school effectiveness research is generally recognized to have been a reaction to the deterministic interpretation of findings by the US researchers Coleman et al. (1966) and Jencks et al. (1972) and, in particular, their pessimistic view of the potential influence of schools, teachers and education on students' achievement (Rutter et al., 1979; Mortimore et al., 1988a; Mortimore, 1993; Reynolds and Creemers, 1990; and Firestone, 1991). These studies indicated that, although background factors are important, schools can have a significant impact. More recently Creemers et al. (1994) have also pointed to the existence of different interpretations reflecting the intellectual ancestries of the school effectiveness research traditions in other national contexts. For example, in the Netherlands interest in school effectiveness grew out of research traditions concerning matters such as teaching, instruction, curriculum and school organization, while in Australia the strong field of educational administration provided a stimulus.

The last 15 years has witnessed a rapid growth in the two related (albeit at times tenuously) areas of research and practice covering the fields of school effectiveness and improvement. In 1990, in a mission statement launching the first issue of a new journal devoted to these topics, Reynolds and Creemers (1990) argued that interest in the topics of school effectiveness and improvement had been 'fuelled by the central place that educational quality (and sometimes equity) issues have assumed in the policy concerns of most developed and many developing societies' (Reynolds and Creemers, 1990: 1).

This review focuses primarily upon the results of school effectiveness research, but it is recognized that many school effectiveness researchers are profoundly concerned about the implications of their work for policy-makers, schools and their students. An interest in raising standards in the widest sense, improving the quality of education and opportunities available to students in all schools, and the implications of research results for practitioners is evident. It is, however, important to recognize that school effectiveness research results do not provide a blueprint or recipe for the creation of more effective schools (Reid et al., 1987; Sammons, 1987; Mortimore et al., 1988a; Creemers, 1994; and Sammons, 1994). School improvement efforts require a particular focus on the processes of change and understanding of the history and context of specific institutions (see Louis and Miles, 1991; Fullan, 1991; Ainscow and West, 1994; and Stoll and Fink, 1994). Whilst it is recognized that, 'in many ways our knowledge of what makes a "good" school greatly exceeds our knowledge of how to apply that knowledge in programmes of school improvement to make schools "good"' (Reynolds and Creemers, 1990: 2), there is growing acceptance that such research provides a valuable background and useful insights for those concerned with improvement (Reid et al. 1987; Mortimore, 1991a and 19911b; Sammons, 1987 and 1994; and Stoll and Fink, 1994). The findings should not, however, be applied mechanically and without reference to a school's particular context. Rather, they can be seen as a helpful starting point for school self-evaluation and review.

Aims and goals of effectiveness research

In reviewing early school effectiveness studies in the US context, Firestone (1991) highlighted the wide ranging impact of studies by Edmonds (1979) and Goodlad et al. (1979). He noted that the effective schools movement was committed to the belief that children of the urban poor could succeed in school and that the school could help them succeed. Firestone (1991) recognized that 'Effectiveness is not a neutral term. Defining the effectiveness of a particular school always requires choices among competing values' and that 'criteria of effectiveness will be the subject of political debate' (Firestone, 1991: 2). Early school effectiveness research incorporated explicit aims or goals concerned with equity and excellence. Three important features were:

- clientele (poor/ethnic minority children)
- subject matter (basic skills in reading and maths)
- equity (children of the urban poor should achieve at the same level as those of the middle class).

This early research therefore, had a limited and specific focus. As Ralph and Fennessey (1983) note, such research was often dominated by the perspectives of school improvers and providers of external support to schools. More recent research, especially in the UK context, has moved away from an explicit equity definition towards a focus on the achievements of all students and a concern with the concept of progress over time rather than cross-sectional 'snapshots' of achievement at a given point in time. This broadens the clientele to include all students, not just the disadvantaged, and a wider range of outcomes (academic and social). As in the US, however, the majority of UK studies have also been conducted in inner city schools. More recent research also recognizes the crucial importance of school intake and attempts to control, usually statistically, for intake differences between schools before any comparisons of effectiveness are made (Mortimore, 1991b; and Mortimore et al., 1995).

Definitions of effectiveness

Although Reid et al. concluded that 'while all reviews assume that effective schools can be differentiated from ineffective ones there is no consensus yet on just what constitutes an effective school' (Reid et al.,

1987: 22), there is now a much greater degree of agreement amongst school researchers concerning appropriate methodology for such studies, about the need to focus explicitly on student outcomes and, in particular, on the concept of the 'value added' by the school (McPherson, 1992). For example, Mortimore (1991a) has defined an effective school as one in which students progress further than might be expected from consideration of its intake. An effective school thus adds extra value to its students' outcomes in comparison with other schools serving similar intakes. By contrast, in an ineffective school students make less progress than expected given their characteristics at intake. Methodological developments have drawn attention to the need to consider issues of consistency and stability in effectiveness and the importance of caution in interpreting any estimates of an individual school's effects. In particular, the need to take account of the confidence limits associated with such estimates is highlighted (Goldstein et al., 1993; Creemers, 1994; Sammons et al., 1994b; and Mortimore et al., 1995).

Definitions of school effectiveness are thus dependent upon a variety of factors as Sammons (1994) has argued. These include:

- sample of schools examined (many studies have focused on inner city schools and this context may affect the general applicability of results)

- choice of outcome measures (studies which focus on only one or two outcomes may give only a partial picture of effectiveness, both in terms of effects and the correlates of effectiveness) a broad range reflecting the aims of schooling being desirable (e.g. the Mortimore et al., 1988a, study examined several cognitive measures and a range of social/affective outcomes)

- adequate control for differences between schools in intakes to ensure that 'like is compared with like' (ideally, information about individual pupils, including baseline measures of prior attainment, personal, socio-economic and family characteristics are required, see Gray et al., 1990; Willms, 1992; Goldstein et al., 1993; Thomas and Mortimore, 1994; and Sammons et al., 1994b)

- methodology (value-added approaches focusing on progress over time and adopting appropriate statistical techniques such as multilevel modelling to obtain efficient estimates of schools' effects and their attached confidence limits are needed, see Goldstein, 1987; Willms and Raudenbush, 1989; Gray et al., 1993; and Goldstein et al., 1993)

- timescale (longitudinal approaches following one or more age cohorts over a period of time rather than cross sectional 'snapshots' are necessary for the study of schools' effects on their students) to allow issues of stability and consistency in schools' effects from year to year to be addressed (see Gray et al., 1993; and Sammons et al., 1993a).

Evidence of effectiveness

The central focus of school effectiveness research concerns the idea that 'schools matter, that schools do have major effects upon children's development and that, to put it simply, schools do make a difference' (Reynolds and Creemers, 1990: 1). Although Preece (1989) looked at research pitfalls of school effectiveness studies and made a number of criticisms of selected studies, Tabberer (1994) concludes that despite Preece's critique there is little argument now that schools can and do have an effect.

During the last two decades, a considerable body of research evidence has accumulated which shows that, although the ability and family backgrounds of students are major determinants of achievement levels, schools in similar social circumstances can achieve very different levels of educational progress (e.g. Reynolds, 1976 and 1982; Gray, 1981; Edmonds, 1979; Brookover et al., 1979; Madaus et al., 1979; Rutter et al., 1979; Mortimore et al., 1988b; Tizard et al., 1988; Smith and Tomlinson, 1989; Willms and Raudenbush, 1989; Nuttall et al., 1989; Gray et al., 1990; Daly, 1991; Fitz-Gibbon, 1991; Jesson and Gray, 1991; Stringfield et al., 1992; Goldstein et al., 1993; Sammons et al., 1994a, 1994b and 1994c; Thomas and Mortimore, 1994; and Thomas et al., 1994). Such studies, conducted in a variety of different contexts, on different age groups and in different countries confirm the existence of both statistically and educationally significant differences between schools in students' achievements.

Most school effectiveness studies have focused on academic achievement in terms of basic skills in reading and mathematics, or examination results (Goodlad, 1984). However, a few have also provided evidence of important differences in social/affective outcomes such as attendance, attitudes and behaviour (Reynolds, 1976; Rutter et al., 1979; and Mortimore et al., 1988a).

There is some indication from recent British research (Sammons et al., 1994a; and Goldstein and Sammons, 1995) following up the *School Matters* cohort that primary school effects may be larger than those identified in the secondary sector, and that primary schools can have a significant long-term impact on later attainment at GCSE (in other words, evidence of a continuing primary school effect). In this connection, Teddlie and Virgilio's (1988) research in the US, which indicates that the variance in teacher behaviour at the elementary grade levels is greater than that at the secondary level, may be relevant.

Measuring effectiveness

Methodological advances, particularly the development of multilevel techniques (e.g. Goldstein, 1987) have led to improvements in the estimation of school effects (Scheerens, 1992; and Creemers, 1994). These have enabled researchers to take better account of differences between schools in the characteristics of their pupil intakes and facilitated exploration of issues such as consistency and stability in schools' effects upon different kinds of outcome and over time (see reviews by Gray et al., 1993; Sammons et al., 1993a; Reynolds et al., 1994; Thomas and Mortimore, 1994; and Mortimore et al., 1995). The need to examine subject differences, whether at A Level (FitzGibbon, 1991 and 1992; and Tymms, 1992) or at GCSE (Sammons et al., 1994c), as well as overall levels of attainment in terms of total A Level or GCSE points scores, is becoming an important focus of recent studies. These highlight the importance of multilevel analyses which examine departmental as well as school effects (see also Dutch work by Luyten, 1994; and Witziers, 1994).

In addition, multilevel techniques also allow investigation of the concept of differential effectiveness, whether some schools are more or less effective for particular student groups (boys or girls, low or high ability students, those from specific ethnic groups).

Issues such as stability and consistency in effects over time and across multiple outcomes, departmental differences and differential effectiveness for particular student groups clearly have important implications for interpreting the effectiveness of individual schools (Nuttall et al., 1989; and Sammons et al., 1993b). Thus, Tabberer, discussing the possibilities of differential effectiveness, notes that 'It is important for, if it exists to a notable extent, then single feature measures of school effectiveness such as are considered for league tables are brought further into question' (Tabberer, 1994).

The importance of taking note of the confidence limits attached to estimates (residuals) which give a measure of the relative value added to or subtracted from their students' achievements by individual schools, also has implications for the use of league tables. It is not appropriate to produce detailed rankings of value-added estimates because the confidence limits overlap (Goldstein et al., 1993; Sammons et al., 1993b, 1994b and 1994c; and Thomas and Mortimore, 1994). Rather, the methodology allows the identification of schools where results are significantly different from those predicted on the basis of intake over one or more years.

Size and importance of school effects

The increasing sophistication of school effectiveness research has provided strong evidence that individual student background characteristics account for a much larger proportion of the total variance in students' academic outcomes than does the particular school attended (Coleman et al., 1966; and Jencks et al., 1972). This is especially true of the impact of prior attainment. However, gender, socio-economic, ethnicity and language characteristics (which, of course are also strongly correlated with prior attainment – see Sammons et al., 1993) also have a small but continuing influence. Creemers (1994) states that 'About 12 to 18 per cent of the variance in student outcomes can be explained by school and classroom factors when we take account the background of the students' (Creemers, 1994: 13). Other authors have produced slightly more modest estimates (between 8 and 10 per cent, Daly, 1991). Expressed as percentages, school and classroom effects do not appear exceptionally large, but in terms of differences between schools in students' outcomes they can be highly significant both educationally and statistically. For example, Thomas and Mortimore (1994) report differences between schools' value-added scores of between 7 grade E results and 7 grade C results (over 14 points) at GCSE.

Whilst there are strong arguments against producing detailed rankings or league tables of schools results even using value-added techniques (Goldstein et al., 1993), the size of the differences between schools identified as statistically significantly more or less effective is not trivial and can be striking (Mortimore et al., 1988b; Gray et al., 1990; and Sammons et al., 1993b and 1994b). Furthermore, Mortimore et al., (1988a and 1988b) have shown that in terms of pupil progress (the value added) school effects are much more important than background factors such as age, gender and social class (being roughly four times more important for reading progress and ten times for mathematics progress). In terms of equity differences, this study also showed that, although no school removed social class differences in attainment, the absolute achievement in basic skills of working class pupils in the most effective schools was higher than those of middle-class pupils in the least effective schools after three years of junior education. Again, such findings point to the educational significance of differences between schools in their effectiveness in adding value to student outcomes, and highlight the importance of using longitudinal rather than cross-sectional approaches.

There is also some evidence from US, UK and Dutch studies that schools' effects may vary for different kinds of outcomes, being larger for subjects such as maths or science primarily taught at school, than for reading or English which are more susceptible to home influences (Scheerens, 1992). Fuller and Clarke's (1994) review of school effects in developing countries reaches similar conclusions.

Unfortunately, less attention has been paid to social than to the academic affective outcomes of education. Further research on these is needed focusing on questions of consistency, stability and differential effectiveness (Sammons et al., 1993).

Context and transferability

There is increasing recognition that, although much can be learned from international and comparative studies of school and teacher effectiveness conducted in different countries, the results of such studies are unlikely to be directly transferable to other contexts (see the discussion by Wimpleberg et al., 1989). For example, early results from the on-going International School Effectiveness Research Programme (ISERP) investigating primary mathematics achievement, provide indications of differences between five countries in the impact of pupil background factors and the effects of certain aspects of teacher behaviour (Creemers et al.,1994). Although, the sample size is severely limited, this research also suggests that the proportion of variance in achievement attributable to schools and classes may vary in different countries.

Creemers (1994) reports findings which point to the contingent nature of school effectiveness research and the importance of distinctions such as primary/secondary and high versus low socio-economic status (SES) of student intakes. Riddell et al. (1994) likewise draw attention to factors such as policy context (national and local) and SES context in case studies of Scottish secondary schools. Reynolds's (1994) international review of school effectiveness research has also highlighted differences in traditions and findings, and the importance of awareness of the contextual dimension of national educational context, which is often subject to rapid change. Fuller and Clarke (1994) likewise draw attention to the importance of context in attempts to analyse school effects in developing countries.

Given the likely importance of contextual factors, particularly national context, the present review has given a particular emphasis to the results of UK school effectiveness research because this is likely to be of greatest relevance to schools in the UK. Other research has also been examined and summarized and, where appropriate, attention is drawn to any differences in the emphasis given to specific findings.

It now widely recognized that there is no simple combination of factors which can produce an effective school (Willms, 1992; and Reynolds and Cuttance, 1992). Indeed, there is very little research 'especially in Britain, which is explicit about "turning round" so-called "ineffective" schools' as Gray and Wilcox (1994) note. These authors go on to argue that:

> in the search for the correlates of effectiveness, the correlates of ineffectiveness have been assumed to be the same. It is by no means clear, however, that they are. How an 'ineffective' school improves may well differ from the ways in which more effective schools maintain their effectiveness.
>
> (Gray and Wilcox, 1994: 2)

Sammons et al. (1994c) have drawn attention to the need for further case studies of ineffective as well as of more effective schools to enhance our understanding of the processes of effectiveness. Recipes for success and 'quick fixes' are not supported by the research base. In contrast to the ambitiously entitled US department review, it is not intended to present deterministic conclusions about 'what works' in education. In many ways every school is unique, 'each has its own characteristics which are shaped by such factors as its location, pupil intake, size, resources and, most importantly, the quality of its staff' (Reid et al., 1987). To this list we can add its particular history, as well as governing body, local education authority and national influences. As Chubb argues,

> school performance is unlikely to be significantly improved by any set of measures that 'fails to recognize that schools are institutions, complex organisations composed of interdependent parts, governed by well established rules and norms of behaviour, and adapted for stability'
>
> (Chubb, 1988).

Nonetheless, given these reservations, a number of reviewers, ourselves included, have identified certain common features concerning the processes and characteristics of more effective schools (e.g. Purkey and

Smith, 1983; Reid et al., 1987; United States Department of Education, 1987; Gray, 1990; North West Regional Education Laboratory, 1990; Firestone, 1991; and Mortimore, 1991a, 1991b and 1993). As Firestone observed:

> There is a core of consistency to be found across a variety of studies conducted here and abroad with a wide range of different methodological strengths and weaknesses. Moreover, there is considerable support for the key findings in related research on organizational behaviour in a variety of work settings and countries.
>
> (Firestone, 1991: 9)

Key characteristics of effective schools

In this section we provide a description of some of the key factors (or correlates) of effectiveness identified by our review. These factors should not be regarded as independent of each other and we draw attention to various links between them which may help to provide a better understanding of possible mechanisms of effectiveness. Whilst our list is not intended to be exhaustive, it provides a summary of relevant research evidence which we hope will provide a useful background for those concerned with promoting school effectiveness and improvement and the processes of school self-evaluation and review.

Professional leadership

Almost every single study of school effectiveness has shown both primary and secondary leadership to be a key factor. Gray has argued that 'the importance of the headteacher's leadership is one of the clearest of the messages from school effectiveness research' (Gray, 1990). He draws attention to the fact that no evidence of effective schools with weak leadership has emerged in reviews of effectiveness research. Reviews by Purkey and Smith (1983) and the United States Department of Education (1987) conclude that leadership is necessary to initiate and maintain school improvement.

However, the importance of the headteacher's leadership role (rather than that of other staff members such as heads of department) may be sensitive to context, particularly patterns of school organization (see Hallinger and Leithwood, 1994). Thus, the headteacher's leadership is a marked feature of British (e.g. Rutter et al., 1979; Mortimore et al., 1988a; Caul, 1994; and Sammons et al., 1994c) and American research (e.g. Edmonds, 1979; Brookover et al., 1979; and Stringfield and Teddlie, 1987), but specific aspects (assertive principal leadership and quality monitoring) have not been found important in the Netherlands (Scheerens, 1992). Hallinger and Leithwood (1994) have argued for further comparative research in this domain.

Leadership is not simply about the quality of individual leaders although this is, of course, important. It is also about the role that leaders play, their style of management, their relationship to the vision, values and goals of the school, and their approach to change.

Looking at the research literature as a whole, it would appear that different styles of leadership can be associated with effective schools, and a very wide range of aspects of the role of leaders in schools have been highlighted. As Bossert et al. concluded, 'no simple style of management seems appropriate for all schools ... principals must find the style and structures most suited to their own local situation' (Bossert et al., 1982: 38). However, a study of the literature reveals that three characteristics have frequently been found to be associated with successful leadership:

1. strength of purpose

2. involving other staff in decision-making

3. professional authority in the processes of teaching and learning.

Firm and purposeful

Effective leadership is usually firm and purposeful. Although case studies have shown isolated examples of schools where the central leadership role is played by another individual, most have shown the headteacher (or principal in US studies) to be the key agent bringing about change in many of the factors affecting school effectiveness (Gray, 1990; and United States Department of Education, 1987).

The research literature shows that outstanding leaders tend to be proactive. For example, effectiveness is enhanced by 'vigorous selection and replacement of teachers' (Levine and Lezotte, 1990), although research in Louisiana (Stringfield and Teddlie, 1987) emphasized that this mainly takes place in the early years of a principal's term or of an improvement drive. Once a staff has been constituted that is capable of working together towards effectiveness, staff stability tends to be resumed in effective secondary schools. Interim results reported by Sammons et al. (1994c) also suggest that in effective schools, heads place a great emphasis on recruitment and also point to the importance of consensus and unity of purpose in the school's senior management team.

Another aspect of firm leadership is brokerage, the ability to mediate or 'buffer' the school from unhelpful change agents, to challenge and even violate externally-set guidelines (Levine and Lezotte, 1990; and Hopkins et al., 1994). The increasing autonomy of schools in recent years has reduced the need for this type of activity, but it has increased the scope for another factor in effective leadership which some studies have shown to be important, namely successful efforts to obtain additional resources, for example through grants or contributions from local business and the community (Venezky and Winfield, 1979; North West Regional Educational Laboratory, 1990; Murphy, 1989; and Levine and Lezotte, 1990).

A number of studies have pointed to the key role of leadership in initiating and maintaining the school improvement process (Trisman et al., 1976; Berman and McLaughlin, 1977; Brookover and Lezotte, 1979; Venezky and Winfield, 1979; Lightfoot, 1983; Louis and Miles, 1992; Stoll and Fink, 1994; and Sammons et al., 1994c). Improving many of the school effectiveness factors or making fundamental changes may require support from outside agencies, such as local education authorities, universities or consultants (Purkey and Smith, 1983; and Weindling, 1989) and successful leaders will establish and sustain regular contact with these networks (Louis and Miles, 1990). However, the message from school improvement programmes, synthesized most exhaustively by Fullan (1991), is that effective change comes from within a school.

Whilst some case studies have pointed to the long hours worked by

Eleven factors for effective schools

1. Professional leadership

    Firm and purposeful
    A participative approach
    The leading professional

2. Shared vision and goals

    Unity of purpose
    Consistency of practice
    Collegiality and collaboration

3. A learning environment

    An orderly atmosphere
    An attractive working environment

4. Concentration on
    teaching and learning

    Maximization of learning time
    Academic emphasis
    Focus on achievement

5. Purposeful teaching

    Efficient organization
    Clarity of purpose
    Structured lessons
    Adaptive practice

6. High expectations

    High expectations all round
    Communicating expectations
    Providing intellectual challenge

7. Positive reinforcement

    Clear and fair discipline
    Feedback

8. Monitoring progress

    Monitoring pupil performance
    Evaluating school performance

9. Pupil rights and responsibilities

    Raising pupil self-esteem
    Positions of responsibility
    Control of work

10. Home–school partnership

    Parental involvement in their
    children's learning

11. A learning organization

    School-based staff development

effective principals (Venezky and Winfield, 1979; and Levine and Stark, 1981), the impact of this factor is difficult to determine. It is *only* effective when accompanied by other factors. It can fluctuate widely over short periods of time and it is almost impossible to separate its direct impact on improvement from its role as a means of building a shared vision and as a signal of ethos to other staff.

A participative approach

A second feature of effective headteachers is the sharing of leadership responsibilities with other members of the senior management team and the involvement more generally of teachers in decision-making. Mortimore et al. (1988a), in their study of primary schools mentioned, in particular, the involvement of the deputy head in policy decisions, the involvement of teachers in management and curriculum planning, and consultation with teachers about spending and other policy decisions, as all being correlates of school effectiveness. This is tied to another important characteristic of a school: the extent to which its culture is a collaborative one (see 'Shared vision and goals').

In larger primary schools and secondary schools, there may be an even greater need for delegation of some of the responsibilities of leadership. Smith and Tomlinson (1989) in their study of secondary schools stressed the importance of leadership and management by heads of departments, a finding which has been borne out by recent research showing substantial differentials in departmental effectiveness within schools (Sammons et al., 1994). In case studies of schools in Northern Ireland, Caul (1994) drew attention both to the need for clear leadership and delegated authority. His study noted the importance of good middle managers in the school at head of department level. Research in the Netherlands has also pointed to the importance of the departmental level in secondary schools (Luyten, 1994; and Witziers, 1994).

Summing up these first two features, effective leadership requires clarity, avoidance of both autocratic and over-democratic ways of working, careful judgement of when to make an autonomous decision and when to involve others, and recognition of the efficacy of the leadership role at different levels of the school. Such leadership is also important for the development and maintenance of a common school mission and a climate of shared goals (see the discussion under 'Shared vision and goals').

The leading professional

An effective headteacher is in most cases not simply the most senior administrator or manager, but is in some sense a leading professional. This implies involvement in and knowledge about what goes on in the classroom, including the curriculum, teaching strategies and the monitoring of pupil progress (Rutter et al., 1979; and Mortimore et al., 1988a). In practice, this requires the provision of a variety of forms of support to teachers, including both encouragement and practical assistance (Levine and Stark, 1981; and Murphy, 1989). It also involves the headteacher projecting a 'high' profile through actions such as frequent movement through the school, visits to the classroom and informal conversation with staff (Sizemore et al., 1983; Mortimore et al., 1988a; Pollack et al., 1987; and Teddlie et al., 1989). It also requires assessment of the ways teachers function, described by Scheerens (1992) as 'one of the pillars of educational leadership'. Of course, this type of approach in itself can have little bearing on effectiveness. It is when it is in conjunction with other factors mentioned, such as emphasis on teaching and learning and regular monitoring throughout the school, that it can have such a powerful impact. Indeed, every one of the 11 key factors that we have identified have implications for effective leaders. This is borne out in Murphy's (1989) distillation of the literature on instructional leadership. The impact headteachers have on student achievement levels and progress is likely to operate indirectly rather than directly by influencing school and staff culture, attitudes and behaviour which, in turn, affect classroom practices and the quality of teaching and learning.

Shared vision and goals

Research has shown that schools are more effective when staff build consensus on the aims and values of the school, and where they put this into practice through consistent and collaborative ways of working and of decision-making. For example, Lee et al.'s (1993) review of literature concerning the organization of effective secondary schools points to the importance of a sense of community 'Such elements of community as cooperative work, effective communication, and shared goals have been identified as crucial for all types of successful organizations, not only schools' (Lee et al., 1993: 227). Others have reached similar conclusions concerning primary schools (e.g. Cohen, 1983; and Mortimore et al., 1988a). Whilst the extent to which this is possible is partly in the hands of the headteacher (see leadership), it also relates to broader features of schools which are not necessarily determined by particular individuals.

Unity of purpose

Most studies of effective organizations emphasize the importance of shared vision in uplifting aspirations and fostering a common purpose. This is particularly important in schools which are challenged to work towards a number of difficult and often conflicting goals, often under enormous external pressure (Purkey and Smith 1983; and Levine and Lezotte 1990). Both school effectiveness research and evaluations of school improvement programmes show that consensus on the values and goals of the school is associated with improved educational outcomes (Trisman et al., 1976; Rutter et al., 1979; Venezky and Winfield, 1979; Lightfoot, 1983; MacKenzie, 1983; Lipsitz, 1984; California Assembly Office of Research, 1984; United States Department of Education, 1987; and Stoll and Fink, 1994). Rutter et al. (1979) stressed that the atmosphere of a school 'will be greatly influenced by the degree to which it functions as a coherent whole' and they found that a school-wide set of values was conducive to both good morale and effective teaching. Similarly, Edmonds (1979) emphasized the importance of school-wide policies and agreement amongst teachers in their aims. Unity of purpose, particularly when it is in combination with a positive attitude towards learning and towards the pupils, is a powerful mechanism for effective schooling (California, 1980). Cohen (1983) has also highlighted the need for clear, public and agreed instructional goals.

In their discussion of Catholic schools' relatively greater effectiveness in promoting students' academic and social outcomes (e.g. low drop out) in the US context, Lee et al. (1993) draw attention to the importance of strong institutional norms and shared beliefs producing an 'educational philosophy that is well aligned with social equity aims' (Lee et al., 1993: 230–1). In Northern Ireland, Caul (1994) has also concluded that more effective schools share common goals including a commitment to quality in all aspects of school life and clear sets of organizational priorities.

Consistency of practice

Related to the notion of consensus amongst staff is the extent to which teachers follow a consistent approach to their work and adhere to common and agreed approaches to matters such as assessment, and the enforcement of rules and policies regarding rewards and sanctions. (See also the discussions concerning 'Positive reinforcement' and 'Monitoring progress'.) Of course, consistency across the school will be much more amenable in a context underpinned by unity of purpose as noted above. Work by Cohen (1983) concludes that the need for curriculum and instructional programmes to be interrelated, especially in elementary (primary) schools, implies that in more effective schools, prevailing norms which grant considerable autonomy to individual teachers carry less weight than do the shared goals of professional staff.

Mortimore et al. (1988a) found that in schools where teachers adopt a consistent approach to the use of school curriculum guidelines there was a positive impact on the progress of pupils. Glenn (1981) had similar findings. Rutter et al. (1979) focused in particular on consistent approaches to discipline and demonstrated that pupils are more likely to maintain principles and guidelines of behaviour when they understand the standards of discipline to be based on 'general expectations set by the school' rather than the whim of the individual teacher. The authors also pointed to the importance of teachers acting as positive role models for the pupil, in their relationships with pupils and other staff and in their attitude to the school. In his study of Welsh secondary schools Reynolds (1976) also drew attention to the importance of avoiding a rigid and coercive approach to discipline.

Collegiality and collaboration

Collegiality and collaboration are important conditions for unity of purpose (Rutter et al., 1979; Lightfoot, 1983; Purkey and Smith, 1983; Lipsitz, 1984; and United States Department of Education, 1987). As was seen in the section on leadership, effective schools tend to have a strong input from staff into the way that the school is run. For example, Rutter et al. (1979) found that pupil success was greater in schools with a decision-making process in which all teachers felt that their views were represented and seriously considered. In the primary sector Mortimore et al. (1988a) also drew attention to the importance of teacher involvement in decision-making and the development of school guidelines creating a sense of 'ownership'. However, such involvement represents only one aspect of collegiality. To some extent, the contribution to achievement comes through a strong sense of community among staff and pupils, fostered through reciprocal relationships of support and respect (Rutter et al., 1979; Wynne, 1980; Lightfoot, 1983; Finn, 1984; Lipsitz, 1984; and Wilson and Corcoran, 1988). It also comes through staff sharing ideas, observing each other and giving feedback, learning from each other, and working together to improve the teaching programme (North West Regional Educational Laboratory, 1990).

A learning environment

The ethos of a school is partly determined by the vision, the values and the goals of the staff, and the way that they work together, as discussed earlier. It is also determined by the climate in which the pupils work: the learning environment. The particular features of this appear to be an orderly atmosphere and an attractive working environment.

An orderly atmosphere

Successful schools are more likely to be calm rather than chaotic places. Many studies have stressed the importance of maintaining a task-oriented, orderly climate in schools (Weber, 1971; Stallings and Hentzell, 1978; Brookover et al., 1979; Edmonds, 1979 and 1981; Rutter et al., 1979; Coleman et al., 1982; and Lightfoot, 1983). Mortimore et al. (1988a) also pointed to the encouragement of self-control amongst pupils as a source of a positive ethos in the classroom, and the disadvantages of high levels of pupil noise and movement for pupil concentration. What the research in general shows is not that schools become more effective as they become more orderly, but rather that an orderly environment is a prerequisite for effective learning to take place. Creemers (1994) also reports on Dutch research by Schwietzer (1984) which concluded that an orderly atmosphere aimed at the stimulation of learning was related to students' academic achievement. The most effective way of encouraging order and purpose amongst pupils is through reinforcement of good practice of learning and behaviour (see also 'Positive reinforcement').

An attractive working environment

School effectiveness research suggests that the physical environment of a school can also have an effect on both the attitudes and achievement of pupils. Rutter et al. (1979) found that keeping a school in a good state of repair and maintenance resulted in higher standards of academic attainment and behaviour, and other studies have shown similar effects (Pablant and Baxter, 1975; and Chan, 1979). Rutter (1983) suggested two explanations for this:

1. attractive and stimulating working conditions tend to improve morale

2. neglected buildings tend to encourage vandalism.

At the primary level, Mortimore et al. (1988a) have also pointed to the importance of creating a pleasant physical environment, including the display of children's work.

Concentration on teaching and learning

The primary purposes of schools concern teaching and learning. These would appear to be obvious activities in an effective school but research suggests that schools differ greatly in the extent to which they concentrate on their primary purpose. Cohen (1983) noted that school effectiveness is clearly dependent upon effective classroom teaching. Similar conclusions about the importance of teaching and learning at the classroom level are evident in reviews by Scheerens (1992), Mortimore (1993) and Creemers (1994). A number of studies have shown correlations between focus on teaching and learning and school and teacher effectiveness. In some cases, this focus has been defined by quantifying teachers' and pupils' use of time, and in others it has been defined in terms of other measures of the school's concentration on the actual process of learning and on achievement. Clearly, it is vital for schools and teachers to focus on the quality as well as the quantity of teaching and learning which takes place.

Maximization of learning time

Some studies have examined the use of time in schools and a number of measures of learning time have been shown to have positive correlations with pupil outcomes and behaviour. The measures include:

- proportion of the day devoted to academic subjects (Coleman et al., 1981) or to particular academic subjects (Bennett, 1978)

- proportion of time in lessons devoted to learning (Brookover et al., 1979; Brookover and Lezotte, 1979; Rutter et al., 1979; and Sizemore, 1987) or to interaction with pupils (Mortimore et al., 1988a; and Alexander, 1992)

- proportion of teachers' time spent discussing the content of work with pupils as opposed to routine matters and the maintenance of work activity (Galton and Simon, 1980; Mortimore et al., 1988a; and Alexander, 1992)

- teachers' concern with cognitive objectives rather than personal relationships and affective objectives (Evertson et al., 1980)

- punctuality of lessons (Rutter et al, 1979; and deJong, 1988)

- freedom from disruption coming from outside the classroom (California, 1980; and Hersch et al., 1981).

Collectively, they point to the need for teachers to manage the transition of activities actively and efficiently. Each of these factors has been seen to have a positive relationship with school effectiveness. Researchers who have combined these variables into a single measure of instruction or academic learning time (Rosenshine and Berliner, 1978; Good, 1984; and Carroll, 1989) or those who have reviewed this literature as a whole (United States Department of Education, 1987; NREL, 1990; and Levine and Lezotte, 1990) have also demonstrated a clear impact of the maximization of learning time on effectiveness. Of course, measures of time provide only a crude indication of focus on learning. As Carroll cautioned 'time as such is not what counts, but what happens during that time' (Carroll, 1989: 27), nonetheless academic learning time and time on task remain powerful predictors of achievement.

In a recent review of British literature on teaching and learning processes, Sammons et al. (1994d) drew attention to findings concerning single-subject teaching and the management of teaching and learning time:

> teachers can have great difficulties in successfully managing children's learning in sessions where work on several different curriculum areas is ongoing. In particular, lower levels of work-related teacher–pupil communication and more routine administrative interactions and lower levels of pupil engagement in work activity have been reported in primary school research studies.
>
> (Sammons et al., 1994: 52)

Academic emphasis

A number of studies, including some mentioned previously, have shown effective schools to be characterized by other aspects of academic emphasis: as judged by teachers and pupils (McDill and Rigsby, 1973); through high levels of pupil industry in the classroom (Weber, 1971; and Mortimore et al., 1988a); and through regular setting and marking of homework (Ainsworth and Batten, 1974), with checks by senior staff that this had occurred (Rutter et al., 1979). Reviews (Walberg, 1985;

and United States Department of Education, 1987) have pointed to the importance of both quantity and quality (appropriateness) of homework set as well as the need for good teacher feedback.

Numerous studies of primary schools have also found that unusually effective schools tend to emphasize 'mastery of academic content' as an important aspect of their teaching programmes (Levine and Lezotte, 1990). In Northern Ireland, Caul's (1994) work has drawn attention to the importance of universal entry to GCSE and an emphasis on academic standards in effective schools. Work by Smith and Tomlinson (1989) has also pointed to examination entry policies as a key feature in secondary school effectiveness. Sammons et al. (1994c) reported that academic emphasis (including regular setting and monitoring of homework) and high GCSE entry rates appear to be features of more highly academically effective secondary schools.

An important factor influencing academic emphasis concerns teachers' subject knowledge. For example, Bennett et al. (1994) have clearly demonstrated that, at the primary level, teachers' knowledge of subject content is often limited particularly in areas such as science. Adequate knowledge was seen as a necessary prerequisite (although not in itself a sufficient condition) for effective teaching and learning. In case studies contrasting highly effective and highly ineffective secondary schools, Sammons et al. (1994c) report that the ineffective schools had experienced high staff turnover and severe staff shortages in specialist subjects which were seen to have acted as barriers to effectiveness.

Curriculum coverage is also important. For example, Bennett (1992) has demonstrated wide variations in curriculum coverage both for pupils within the same class and in different schools. Likewise, Tizard et al.'s (1988) work on infant schools pointed to a wide range between schools and classes in what children of the same age were taught which could not be accounted for by intake differences. These researchers emphasized the importance of curriculum coverage: 'it is clear that attainment and progress depend crucially on whether children are given particular learning experiences' (Tizard et al., 1988: 172).

Focus on achievement

Some researchers have examined the extent to which a school concentrates on the achievement of pupils as a measure of academic emphasis. For example, some case studies of US primary schools and reviews have shown emphasis on the acquisition of basic skills or 'achievement orientation' to have a positive influence on school effectiveness (Brookover and Lezotte, 1979; Brookover et al., 1979; Venezky and Winfield, 1979; Glenn, 1981; Edmonds, 1979 and 1981; and Schweitzer, 1984). The problem with highlighting this type of factor is that outcome measures tend to be at least partly based on tests in these skills for primary schools or examination achievement for secondary schools, making factors associated with focus on achievement self-fulfilling prophesies. This is particularly true in relation to class-level data, but less of a problem when examining the effect of a *shared* acceptance of a commitment to a focus on achievement throughout a school.

So while a focus on teaching and learning is at the heart of an effective school, researchers have approached it from a number of different angles. One interesting attempt to consolidate this work is that of Scheerens (1992) who, drawing on a vast range of international school effectiveness literature, judged effective learning time to be one of only three factors for which there is multiple empirical research confirmation. He considered four aspects to be relevant:

1. institutionalized time spent on learning (length of school day/week/ year)

2. amount of homework

3. effective learning time within institutional constraints

4. learning time for different subjects.

Whilst this typology may not entirely capture the essence of 'focus on teaching and learning', it provides a useful framework for pinning down measurable factors that indicate important practical manifestations of this focus.

Purposeful teaching

It is clear from the research literature that the quality of teaching is at the heart of effective schooling. Of course, this is partly determined by the quality of the teachers in the school, and as we have seen, recruiting and replacing teachers is an important role in effective leadership. However, high quality teachers do not always perform to their full potential, and teaching styles and strategies are important factors related to pupil progress. Whereas learning is a covert process and 'not amenable to direct observation', teaching is an overt activity and hence is easier to describe and evaluate (Mortimore, 1993), although Levine and Lezotte (1990) have pointed to a number of problems in drawing general conclusions on effective teaching practices. Examining the findings on teaching practices in effective schools research, the outstanding factor that emerges is what we call purposeful teaching. This has a number of elements: efficient organization, clarity of purpose, structured lessons and adaptive practice.

Efficient organization

Several studies have shown the importance of teachers being well-organized and absolutely clear about their objectives. For example, Evertson et al. (1980) found positive effects on achievement when teachers felt 'efficacy and an internal locus of control', and where they organized their classrooms and planned proactively on a daily basis.

Rutter et al. (1979) drew attention to the beneficial effects of preparing the lesson in advance and Rutter (1983) later pointed out that the more time that teachers spend organising a lesson after it has begun, the more likely it is that they will lose the attention of the class, with the attendant double risk of loss of opportunity to learn and disruptive behaviour. Various studies and reviews have also stressed the importance of appropriate pacing of lessons to make sure that their original objectives are achieved (Powell, 1980; Brophy and Good, 1986; and Levine and Lezotte, 1990).

Clarity of purpose

Syntheses of effective schools research highlight the importance of pupils always being aware of the purpose of the content of lessons (Brophy and Good, 1986; United States Department of Education, 1987; and North West Regional Educational Laboratory, 1990). In summary, the research shows that effective learning occurs where teachers clearly explain the objectives of the lesson at the outset and refer to these throughout the lesson to maintain focus. These objectives should be related to previous study and to things of personal relevance of the pupils. The information of the lesson should be structured such that it begins with an overview and transitions are signalled. The main ideas of the lesson should be reviewed at the end.

Structured lessons

A review by Rosenshine and Stevens (1981) highlighted the importance of structured teaching and purposefulness in promoting pupil progress. The North West Regional Educational Laboratory review (1990) drew particular attention to effective questioning techniques where questions are structured so as to focus pupils' attention on the key elements of the lessons. Stallings (1975) pointed to improvements in pupil outcomes through systematic teaching methods with open-ended questions, pupil answers, followed by teacher feedback. Supporting earlier findings by Galton and Simon (1980), Mortimore et al. (1988a) likewise noted positive effects on progress through teachers spending more time asking questions and on work-related communication in their study of junior education. They also found positive outcomes to be associated with efficient organization of classroom work with plenty for pupils to do, a limited focus to sessions, and a well-defined framework within which a degree of pupil independence and responsibility for managing their own work could be encouraged. Clearly, for older age groups greater stress on independence and responsibility is appropriate.

A summary of research on effective teachers by Joyce and Showers (1988) concludes that the more effective teachers:

- teach the classroom as a whole

- present information or skills clearly and animatedly

- keep the teaching sessions task-oriented

- are non-evaluative and keep instruction relaxed

- have high expectations for achievement (give more homework, pace lessons faster and create alertness)

- relate comfortably to the students, with the consequence that they have fewer behaviour problems.

Scheerens (1992) in his analysis of the international body of effective schools research highlights 'structured teaching' as one of three factors which have been convincingly demonstrated to promote effectiveness. His definition of structured teaching is slightly different from other researchers but it is worth looking at some of the examples of what he means by it:

- making clear what has to be learnt

- splitting teaching material into manageable units for the pupils and offering these in a well-considered sequence

- much exercise material in which pupils make use of 'hunches' and prompts

- regularly testing for progress with immediate feedback of the results.

Scheerens admits that this exemplification of structured teaching is more applicable to primary schools, in particular in subjects that involve 'reproducible knowledge'. However, he suggests that a modified and less prescriptive form of structured teaching can have a positive effect for the learning of higher cognitive processes and in secondary schools, and he cites a number of studies to confirm this (Brophy and Good,

1986; and Doyle, 1985). Gray (1993) is not convinced that this factor is appropriate beyond the earlier years of schooling and he suggests that we need to be cautious, given that so much of the early school effectiveness research is focused on disadvantaged schools thus giving particular weight to the teaching of basic skills.

Adaptive practice

Although school effectiveness research shows a number of factors to be consistently correlated with better outcomes, it also shows that application of mandated curriculum materials and teaching procedures does not often bring out gains in achievement. Pupil progress is enhanced when teachers are sensitive to differences in the learning styles of pupils and, where feasible, identify and use appropriate strategies (North West Regional Educational Laboratory, 1990). In many cases, this requires flexibility on the part of the teachers in modifying and adapting their teaching styles (Armor et al., 1976; and Sizemore et al., 1983).

High expectations

Positive expectations of pupil achievement, particularly amongst teachers but also pupils and parents, is one of the most important characteristics of effective schools (United States Department of Education, 1987). However, care is needed in interpreting the relationship between expectations and achievement, since the causal process can run in the reverse direction, with high achievement enhancing optimism amongst teachers. However, the weight of the evidence suggests that if teachers set high standards for their pupils, let them know that they are expected to meet them and provide intellectually challenging lessons to correspond to these expectations, then the impact on achievement can be considerable. In particular, low expectations of certain kinds of student have been identified as an important factor in the under-achievement of students in disadvantaged urban schools (OFSTED, 1993).

High expectations all round

A large number of studies and review articles in several countries have shown a strong relationship between high expectations and effective learning (Trisman et al., 1976; Brookover et al., 1979; Edmonds, 1979 and 1981; Rutter et al., 1979; California, 1980; Schweitzer, 1984; Stringfield et al., 1986; United States Department of Education, 1987; Tizard et al., 1988; Mortimore et al., 1988a; Scheerens, 1992; Stoll and Fink, 1992; Caul, 1994; and Sammons et al., 1994c). High expectations have also been described as a 'crucial characteristic of virtually all unusually effective schools described in case studies' (Levine and Lezotte, 1990). The important point as far as teachers are concerned is that low expectations go hand in hand with a sense of lack of control over pupils' difficulties and a passive approach to teaching. High expectations correspond to a more active role for teachers in helping pupils to learn (Mortimore, 1994) and a strong sense of efficacy (Armor et al., 1976).

As with most of the factors identified in this report, high expectations alone can do little to raise effectiveness. They are most likely to be operationalized in a context where there is a strong emphasis on academic achievement, where pupils' progress is frequently monitored, and where there is an orderly environment, conducive to learning. In addition, high expectations are more effective when they are part of a general culture which places demands on everyone in the school, so that, for example, the headteacher has high expectations for the performance and commitment of all of the teachers (Murphy, 1989).

Communicating expectations

Expectations do not act directly on pupil performance, but through the attitude of the teacher being communicated to pupils and the consequent effect on their self-esteem (Bandura, 1992). The expectations may be influenced by factors other than the perceived ability or actual attainments of children. For example, Mortimore et al. (1988a) found that teachers had lower expectations for younger pupils in the class and for those from lower social classes, even when account was taken of children's attainment in areas such as reading and mathematics. But even if teachers do not believe success is possible, conveying conviction that achievement can be raised can have a powerful effect. Teachers may need to monitor either or both their beliefs and behaviour to make sure that this takes place (North West Regional Educational Laboratory, 1990). It should also be noted that raising expectations is an incremental process and demonstrated success plays a critical role (Wilson and Corcoran, 1988). Reinforcing this success through praise (see 'Positive reinforcement') is a key opportunity for communicating high expectations.

Providing intellectual challenge

There seems little doubt that a common cause of under-achievement in pupils is a failure to challenge them. The implications of this are that when schools have high expectations of their pupils they attempt, wherever possible, to provide intellectually challenging lessons for all pupils in all classes. This approach has been shown by several studies to be associated with greater effectiveness.

A piece of research in the UK had some important findings which go some way to explaining the processes through which expectations have an effect. Tizard et al. (1988) in a study of infant schools in Inner London found that teachers' expectations of both individual pupils and of classes as a whole had a strong influence on the content of lessons, which to a large extent explained differences in curriculum between classes with similar intakes. These expectations were not just influenced by academic considerations but also by the extent to which a child or a class was 'a pleasure to teach'. The result was that different levels of expectations of pupils were translated into differing requirements for their work and their performance.

Mortimore et al. (1988a) in their study of the junior years of primary schools found that in classes where the pupils were stimulated and challenged, progress was greatest. They particularly mentioned the importance of teachers using more higher-order questions and statements and encouraging pupils 'to use their creative imagination and powers of problem-solving'. Levine and Stark (1981) also stressed the importance of the development of higher-order cognitive skills in effective primary schools, mentioning in particular reading comprehension and problem solving in mathematics. Levine and Lezotte (1990) and North West Regional Educational Laboratory (1990) pointed to a number of other studies with similar findings.

Positive reinforcement

Reinforcement, whether in terms of patterns of discipline or feedback to pupils, is an important element of effective schooling (Brookover et al., 1979; and Rutter et al., 1979). Walberg (1984) in a major review of studies of teaching methods found that reinforcement was the most powerful factor of all. As will be seen, school effectiveness research has tended to show that not all forms of reinforcement have a positive impact. Rewards, other positive incentives and clear rules are more likely than punishment to be associated with better outcomes.

Clear and fair discipline

Good discipline is an important condition for an orderly climate (see ethos), but is best derived from 'belonging and participating' rather than 'rules and external control' (Wayson et al., 1988). For example, too frequent use of punishment can create a tense and negative atmosphere with counterproductive effects on attendance and behaviour (Rutter, 1983). Indeed, a number of studies have found that formal punishments are either ineffective or have adverse effects (Reynolds and Murgatroyd, 1977; Clegg and Megson, 1968; Rutter et al., 1979; Heal, 1978; and Mortimore et al., 1988). These and other studies show that effective discipline involves keeping good order, consistently enforcing fair, clear and well-understood rules and infrequent use of actual punishment (National Institute of Education, 1978; Rutter et al., 1979; and Coleman et al., 1981).

Feedback

Feedback to pupils can be immediate (in the form of praise or reprimand) or to some extent delayed (in the form of rewards, incentives and prizes).

Two large reviews of effective schools research showed that school-wide or public recognition of academic success and of other aspects of positive behaviour contribute to effectiveness (North West Regional Educational Laboratory, 1990; and Purkey and Smith, 1994). The UK study of secondary schools by Rutter et al. (1979) showed that direct and positive feedback such as praise and appreciation had a positive association with pupil behaviour, but that prizes for work had little effect on any outcome measure. The researchers posited three explanations for the greater effect of praise:

1. it affects a greater number of pupils

2. the lack of delay allows more definite links to incentives

3. it is more likely to increase the *intrinsic* rewards of that which is being reinforced.

Mortimore et al. (1988) had similar findings for primary schools showing that praise and indeed neutral feedback were more effective than 'a reliance on control through criticism'. It should be noted that the North West Regional Educational Laboratory synthesis of the literature (1990) pointed out that the research shows that praise and other reinforcements should be provided for correct answers and progress in relation to past performance, but that use should be sparing and must not be unmerited or random. A number of studies have also shown that rewards and praise need not necessarily be related solely to academic outcomes, but can apply to other aspects of school life such as attendance and citizenship (Rutter et al., 1979; Hallinger and Murphy, 1986; and Levine and Lezotte, 1990). Brophy and Good's (1986) review of teacher behaviour and student achievement provides a set of guidelines for effective praise. Amongst other aspects, these stress the need for praise to be specific, contingent, spontaneous and varied and to use students' own prior accomplishments as a context for describing present accomplishments and to attribute success to effort and ability.

Monitoring progress

Well-established mechanisms for monitoring the performance and progress of pupils, classes, the school as a whole, and improvement programmes, are important features of many effective schools. These procedures may be formal or informal, but either way they contribute to a focus on teaching and learning and often play a part in raising expectations and in positive reinforcement. There appear to be particular benefits from active headteacher engagement in the monitoring of pupil achievement and progress.

Monitoring pupil performance

Frequent and systematic monitoring of the progress of pupils and classes by itself has little impact on achievement, but has been shown to be an important ingredient of the work of an effective school (see Weber, 1971; Venezky and Winfield, 1979; Edmonds, 1979 and 1981; and Sizemore, 1985). First, it is a mechanism for determining the extent to which the goals of the school are being realized. Second, it focuses the attention of staff, pupils and parents on these goals. Third, it informs planning, teaching methods and assessment. Fourth, it gives a clear message to pupils that teachers are interested in their progress. This last point relates to teachers giving feedback to pupils, which we discuss under 'positive reinforcement'.

Levine and Lezotte (1990) recognized monitoring of student progress as a factor often cited in effective schools research, but argued that there has been little agreement about defining the term or providing guidance for practice. They also pointed to a number of studies that have shown that some schools waste time or misdirect teaching through too frequent monitoring procedures. In their list of effective school correlates they used the phrase 'appropriate monitoring' in view of the need for more work on the form and frequency of its use.

A large British study of primary schools (Mortimore et al., 1988) concentrated on a well-established form of monitoring pupil performance. These researchers examined record-keeping by teachers as a form of continual monitoring of the strengths and weaknesses of pupils, combining the results of objective assessments with teachers' judgement of their pupils. In many effective schools these records relate not only to academic abilities but also to personal and social development. The researchers found record-keeping to be an important characteristic of effective schools.

Evaluating school performance

Effective schools research also shows that monitoring pupil performance and progress at the school-level is an important factor. In discussing leadership, we already mentioned the importance of the headteacher having active involvement and detailed knowledge of the workings of the school, for example through visiting classrooms. On a more formal basis, Murphy's (1989) review of studies of effective leaders showed that they practice a range of monitoring procedures, feed back their interpretation of these to teachers and integrate these procedures with evaluation and goal-setting.

Scheerens (1992), in a review of school effectiveness research, argued that proper evaluation is 'an essential prerequisite to effectiveness-enhancing measures at all levels'. Evaluating school improvement programmes is particularly important. For example, Lezotte (1989) emphasized the importance of the use of measures of pupil achievement as the basis for programme evaluation, indeed, this was one of his five factors for school effectiveness.

It could be concluded that the feedback and incorporation of monitoring and evaluation information routinely into decision-making procedures in the school ensures that information is used actively. Such information also needs to be related to staff development (see also 'The learning organization').

Pupil rights and responsibilities

A common finding of effective schools research is that there can be quite substantial gains in effectiveness when the self-esteem of pupils is raised, when they have an active role in the life of the school, and when they are given a share of responsibility for their own learning.

Raising pupil self-esteem

Levels of self-esteem are significantly affected by treatment by others and are a major factor determining achievement (Helmreich, 1972; and Bandura, 1992). In the case of pupil self-esteem, the attitudes of teachers are expressed in a number of ways:

- the way that they communicate with pupils

- the extent to which pupils are accorded respect and feel they are understood

- the efforts teachers make to respond to the personal needs of individual pupils.

Trisman et al. (1976) found student–teacher rapport to have a beneficial influence on outcomes, and a number of other studies have shown positive teacher–pupil relations to be a dimension linked with success (Rutter et al., 1979; Coleman et al., 1982; Lightfoot, 1983; and Lipsitz, 1984). Mortimore et al. (1988) found positive effects where teachers communicated enthusiasm to pupils and where they showed interest in children as individuals.

Teacher–pupil relationships can be enhanced out of the classroom. UK studies of secondary schools have found that when there were shared out-of-school activities between teachers and pupils (Rutter et al., 1979; and Smith and Tomlinson, 1990) and where pupils felt able to consult their teachers about personal problems (Rutter et al., 1979), there were positive effects on outcomes.

Positions of responsibility

UK studies have also shown positive effects on both pupil behaviour and examination success through giving a high proportion of children positions of responsibility in the school system, thus conveying trust in pupils' abilities and setting standards of mature behaviour (Ainsworth and Batten, 1974; Reynolds et al., 1976; Reynolds and Murgatroyd, 1977; and Rutter et al., 1979).

Control of work

Some studies have shown that when pupils respond well when they are given greater control over what happens to them at school, enhancing a number outcomes, even at the primary level (NIE, 1978; and Brookover et al., 1979). A UK study of primary schools showed that there are positive effects when pupils are encouraged to manage their work independently of the teacher over short periods of time, such as a lesson or an afternoon (Mortimore et al., 1988).

Home–school partnership

Effective schools research generally shows that supportive relations and cooperation between home and schools have positive effects. Coleman et al. (1993) has drawn particular attention to the benefits of schools fostering parents' involvement in their children's learning. The question of whether higher levels of parental involvement have an impact is a difficult one, since it can mean a multitude of things in different contexts and there are likely to be marked differences between primary and secondary schools in the nature of parental involvement. As yet, there has been no research into the relationship between the level of accountability of schools to parents in the UK (increased under the provisions of the Education Reform Act 1988) and their effectiveness.

Parental involvement in their children's learning

The particular ways in which schools encourage good home–school relations and foster parents' involvement with their children's learning will be affected by the pupils' age and marked differences are likely to be identified between primary and secondary schools.

Mortimore et al.'s (1988a) junior school study found positive benefits where parents helped in the classroom and with school trips, where there were regular progress meetings, where there was a parents' room and where the headteacher had an 'open door' policy. Interestingly, they found a negative effect for parent–teacher associations, and suggested that this more formalized type of parental involvement was not sufficient in itself to engender involvement and in some cases, could present barriers to those not within the 'clique'. Tizard et al. (1982) showed that parental involvement in reading had more effect than an extra teacher in the classroom. Epstein (1987), Weinberger et al. (1990) and Topping (1992) have also drawn attention to the value of parental involvement in reading projects in primary schools.

Armor et al. (1976) showed that parental presence in the school buildings, and participation in committees, events and other activities all had positive effects on achievement. On the other hand, Brookover and Lezotte (1979) found no support for a relationship between parental involvement and effectiveness.

More recent work on school improvement by Coleman (1944) and Coleman et al. (1993 and 1994) has drawn attention to the importance of positive and supportive teacher, student and parent attitudes for the development of student responsibility for learning.

Parental involvement is often highly correlated with socio-economic factors, and concern that highlighting it as an important factor might unfairly pass responsibility for effectiveness to parents partly explains why some researchers have avoided defining or measuring it. However, the studies did control for socio-economic intake. Interestingly, at least one study has shown that parental involvement can be *more effective* in schools enrolling more poor or working-class pupils (Hallinger and Murphy, 1986).

Interim results by Sammons et al. (1994c) indicate that there was a tendency for staff in less effective secondary schools to attribute lack of parental interest as a major factor contributing to under-achievement, whereas in more effective secondary schools serving similar intakes there were more favourably perceptions of parental interest and more active relations with parents.

The actual mechanisms by which parental involvement influences school effectiveness are not entirely clear. It might be speculated that where parents and teachers have similar objectives and expectations for children, the combined support for the learning process can be a powerful force for improvement (Jowett et al., 1991; Mortimore, 1993; and Coleman, 1994). Parents who are involved may expand pupils' active learning time (e.g. by working with children themselves especially for younger children or by supervising homework) and, in the case of difficulties arising at school, perhaps in attendance or behaviour, being more likely to support the school's requirements and standards. As MacBeath (1994) has argued, successful schools are likely to be those 'which not only "involve" but support and make demands on parents' (MacBeath, 1994: 5). He further argues for a more active role for parents in school self-evaluation and development planning. Coleman et al. (1994) draw particular attention to the interconnectedness of the affective and cognitive domains in the triad of relationships between teacher, parent and student. They argue 'it is the relationship between the individual teacher and the parent(s) that is critical in enlisting the home as ally, or rendering it the enemy of the educative (or not) activities of the classroom' (Coleman et al., 1994: 30).

A learning organization

Effective schools are learning organizations, with teachers and senior managers continuing to be learners, keeping up to date with their subjects and with advances in understanding about effective practice. We use the term 'learning organization' in a second sense which is that this learning has most effect when it takes place at the school itself or is school-wide, rather than specific to individual teachers. The need for schools to become 'learning organizations' is increasingly important given the pace of societal and educational change (Hopkins et al., 1994). Southworth (1994) provides a helpful review of the features of a learning school which stresses the need for learning at five interrelated levels – children's, teacher, staff, organizational and leadership learning.

School-based staff development

Almost every single research study which has looked at the impact of staff development on school effectiveness has pointed to the need for it to be school-based. For example, Mortimore et al. (1988a) found that in-service training courses only had a positive effect on outcomes when they were attended for a good reason. Stedman (1987) stressed the importance of training being tailored to the specific needs of staff and being 'an integral part of a collaborative educational environment'. Coleman and LaRocque's (1990) research in Canada also points to the positive impact which support from administrative bodies at a local level (school boards equivalent to local education authorities) can provide.

Levine and Lezotte (1990) and Fullan (1991) cite a number of studies that show that one-off presentations by outside experts can be counterproductive. Their review of unusually effective schools had similar conclusions to other reviews and studies. Staff development in effective schools is generally at the school site, is focused on providing assistance to improve classroom teaching and the instructional programme, and is ongoing and incremental (Armor et al., 1976; Venezky and Winfield, 1979; California, 1980; Glenn, 1981; Purkey and Smith, 1983; Hallinger and Murphy, 1985; and North West Regional Educational Laboratory, 1990). Studies have also stressed the value of embedding staff development within collegial and collaborative planning, and ensuring that ideas from development activities are routinely shared (Purkey and Smith, 1983; North West Regional Educational Laboratory, 1990; and Stoll and Fink, 1994).

Conclusions

The majority of effectiveness studies have focused exclusively on students' cognitive outcomes in areas such as reading, mathematics or public examination results. Only a relatively few (mainly UK) studies have paid attention to social/affective outcomes (e.g. Reynolds, 1976; Rutter, 1979; Mortimore et al., 1988a; and Teddlie and Stringfield, 1993). Because of this focus, the results of our review, inevitably, tell us more about the correlates of academic effectiveness. As Reynolds (1994) has observed, we have less evidence about school and classroom processes that are important in determining schools' success in promoting social or affective outcomes such as behaviour, attendance, attitudes and self-esteem. Barber (1993) has drawn particular attention to the major problem of low levels of pupil motivation in British secondary schools, and combatting this is likely to be especially important for raising standards in deprived urban areas. Further research on the ways effective schools influence social and affective outcomes including student motivation and commitment to school would be desirable. Having said this, we feel that enhancing academic outcomes and fostering pupils' learning and progress remain crucial tests of effective schooling. For this reason, identifying the correlates of effectiveness, especially academic effectiveness has an important part to play in making informed judgements about schools.

The 11 interrelated and, in many ways, mutually dependent factors identified in this review appear to be generic. In other words, evidence for their importance is derived from both secondary and primary school studies. Initially, an attempt was made to produce separate analyses for the two sectors. However, the degree of overlap identified in findings would, in our view, make the presentation of separate summaries repetitious.

Despite the agreement in findings for both sectors, however, it should be noted that the emphasis or means of expression will often differ. For example, the ways in which a school pays attention to the factors 'pupil rights and responsibilities' and 'positive reinforcement' will clearly be strongly influenced by pupils' age. Appropriate forms of praise and reward and the manner and extent to which pupils are encouraged to take responsibility for their own learning and to become involved in the school's life will vary for different age groups. Nonetheless, the need for appropriate feedback and positive reinforcement and a concern with pupil rights and responsibilities is important at all stages in education. Ways of focusing on teaching and learning and teaching techniques will also differ for different age groups, but careful and appropriate planning and organization, clarity of objectives, high quality teaching and maximization of learning time remain crucial for effective teaching at all stages. Likewise, ways of fostering parental involvement in their children's learning and with the school will also vary markedly between the primary and secondary sectors.

The centrality of teaching and learning

Scheerens (1992) has rightly drawn attention to the centrality of teaching and learning and of classroom processes in determining schools' academic effectiveness in particular. The 11 factors identified in this review focus on aspects to do with whole school processes (leadership, decision-making, management, goals, expectations and so on) and those to do with, and directly related to, classroom organization and teaching. Ultimately, the quality of teaching (expressed most clearly by factors 4 and 5) and expectations (factor 6) have the most significant role to play in fostering pupils' learning and progress and, therefore, in influencing their educational outcomes. Given this, school processes, including professional leadership, remain highly influential because they provide the overall framework within which teachers and classrooms operate. They are important for the development of consistent goals and ensuring that pupils' educational experiences are linked as they progress through the school. In some schools (those that are more effective) the overall framework is far more supportive for classroom practitioners and pupil learning than in others.

The results of our review do not support the view that any one particular teaching style is more effective than others. Mortimore et al.'s (1988a) analysis of observational and other data about primary school teachers indicated that teacher behaviour was too complex and varied for the application of simple descriptions of teaching style or approach and that 'teachers could not validly be divided into a number of categories on the basis of differences in teaching style' (Mortimore et al., 1988a: 81). Re-analysis of the Bennett (1976) data by Aitkin et al. (1981) also points to problems in the use of divisions such as 'formal' or 'informal', 'traditional' versus 'progressive' and the separation of teachers into groups operating distinctive styles. Joyce and Showers's (1988) analysis of ways staff development can foster student achievement concludes that a number of educational practices 'ranging across ways of managing students and learning environments, teaching strategies or models of teaching ... can affect student learning' (Joyce and Showers, 1988: 56). Recent reviews highlight the importance of effective management, clarity of objectives, good planning, appropriate and efficient organisation of pupils' time and activities, and emphasis on work communication and intellectually challenging teaching (Gipps, 1992; and Sammons et al.,1994d) and suggest that flexibility, the ability to adapt teaching approaches for different purposes and groups is more important than notions of one single 'style' being better than others. Indeed, in our view, debates about the virtues of one particular teaching style over another are too simplistic and have become sterile. Efficient organization, fitness for purpose, flexibility of approach and intellectual challenge are of greater relevance.

Common sense
The findings of school effectiveness research have sometimes been criticized for being just a matter of 'common sense'. Sammons (1994) notes:

> There is a grain of truth in this argument. Because school effectiveness research by its very nature sets out to identify the components of good practice ... it is inevitable that some of the findings are unsurprising to practitioners.
>
> (Sammons, 1994: 46)

Rutter et al. (1979) likewise pointed out that:

> research into practical issues, such as schooling rarely comes up with findings that are totally unexpected. On the other hand it is helpful in showing which of the abundance of good ideas available are related to successful outcomes.
>
> (Rutter et al., 1979: 204)

In a discussion about appropriate frameworks for judging the quality of schooling, Gray (1990) commented:

> As a rule, schools which do the kinds of things the research suggests make a difference, tend to get better results (however these are measured or assessed). The problem is that these are tendencies not

certainties. In betting terms the research would be right about seven out of ten times, especially if it could be supported by professional assessments.

(Gray, 1994: 214)

In connection with Gray's comments on the importance of professional assessments, it is interesting to note the links between the findings of this review of school effectiveness research and some of the conclusions reached in studies by inspectors. For example, the influential HMI report *Ten Good Schools* (Department of Education and Science Inspectorate of Schools, 1977) explicitly drew attention to common features in a sample of secondary schools judged to be 'good'. This report suggested that:

success does not stem merely from the existence of certain structures of organization, teaching patterns or curriculum planning, but is dependent on the spirit and understanding that pervades the life and work of a school, faithfully reflecting its basic objectives.

(Department of Education and Science Inspectorate of Schools, 1977: 7)

In particular, the creation of a 'well-ordered environment', levels of expectation which are at once realistic and demanding, whether in academic performance or in social behaviour and the need for functions and responsibilities to be clearly defined and accepted were highlighted. Other aspects emphasized include the professional skills of the headteacher, the importance of teamwork, and systems for monitoring progress and pastoral care of students. In connection with the quality of teaching aspects such as variety of approach, regular and constructive correction of work, and consistent encouragement were seen as 'the hallmarks of successful teaching'. School climate, leadership and links with the local community were also noted.

Comparisons with *Ten Good Schools* are useful because this report pre-dates much of the school effectiveness research we have reviewed and, therefore, is less likely to have been influenced by the dissemination of research findings than more recent inspection documents which often refer to the effectiveness research explicitly. The professional judgements evident in this report draw attention to many of the aspects covered by the 11 key factors which have emerged from our review of school effectiveness research.

Resources

Most studies of school effectiveness have not found the level of resources allocated to schools to be a major determinant of effectiveness. However, this does not imply that resources are unimportant. Mortimore et al. (1988a) cautioned that the schools in its sample:

> were all relatively well resourced (under the arrangements of the former ILEA). Because all schools were well funded, we did not find resourcing to be a key factor. Had our sample been drawn from a range of LEAs with both high and low spending traditions, it is unlikely this would have been the case.
>
> (Mortimore et al., 1981: 264)

The importance of a good physical environment of staffing stability and absence of staff shortages were also noted.

Influential US research by Hanushek (1986 and 1989) involving meta-analyses of many studies concluded that there was little relationship between levels of resources and the accomplishments of students in schools, but many of the studies included suffered from significant limitations. A recent re-analysis of Hanushek's synthesis of the literature (using the same set of studies with their limitations) has questioned this view. Hedges et al.'s (1994) re-analysis indicates that the impact of resource allocations (especially per pupil expenditure) has been underestimated. These authors reject Hanushek's conclusion that resources are unrelated to outcomes, noting that 'the question of whether more resources are needed to produce real improvements in our nation's schools can no longer be ignored' (Hedges et al., 1994: 13). Whilst a new appreciation of evidence concerning the positive impact of resources is timely, our review suggests that the aspects of school and classroom processes summarized under the headings of the 11 key factors exert more powerful and direct influences. Our review confirms Gray's (1990) observation that:

> adequate levels of resourcing, then, seem to be necessary but not a
> sufficient condition for a school to be effective ... in twenty years
> of reading research on the characteristics of effective schools I have
> only once come across a record of an 'excellent' school where the
> physical environment left something to be desired.
>
> (Gray, 1990: 213)

Educational markets and other changes

It is important to recognize that the evidence accumulated concerning the correlates of effectiveness during the last 20 years does not allow any firm conclusions to be drawn about the impact of recent legislative changes in the UK which were intended to improve quality and raise standards by extending diversity and choice and stimulate the development of educational markets (Department of Education, 1992). For example, the increased powers and role of governors in school management and the changing role of the headteacher under Local Management of Schools have not, as yet, featured in school effectiveness studies. Similarly, whilst parental involvement has been found to be important, it is not possible as yet to establish the impact of increased choice and availability of greater information (e.g. the publication of league tables) intended to increase accountability on school performance. Further research addressing such changes is require before their impact on schools can be evaluated (Sammons and Hillman, 1994). Other changes in the UK context which are also likely to prove important in future school effectiveness research include the impact of development planning (MacGilchrist, 1995) and the impact of the National Curriculum and national assessment. Many other education systems in different parts of the world have or are in the process of introducing similar kinds of changes to those evident in the UK and studies which explicitly examine the consequences of such changes in context for school effectiveness are urgently needed.

Acknowledgments

Helpful comments on an earlier draft were received from Professor Peter Coleman, Dr David Hopkins, Dr David Jones, Dr Peter Matthews, Professor David Reynolds and Dr Louise Stoll.

6 Peddling feel-good fictions

David Hamilton

Reflections on Sammons, P., Hillman, J. and Mortimore, P. (1995) *Key Characteristics of Effective Schools: A Review of School Effectiveness Research.*

Effective schooling has become an international industry. Its activities embrace four processes: research, development, marketing and sales. Research entails the construction of new prototypes; development entails the commodification of these prototypes; marketing entails the promotion of these commodities; and sales entails the effort to ensure that market returns exceed financial investment. The school effectiveness industry, therefore, stands at the intersection of educational research and a much broader political agenda – social engineering.

There is another perspective on school effectiveness research. Its efforts cloak school practices in a progressive, social-darwinist, eugenic rationale. It is progressive because it seeks more efficient and effective ways of steering social progress. It is social-darwinist because it accepts survival of the fittest. And it is eugenic because it endorses the desirable and, consequently, depreciates the exceptional.

But something else lurks beneath this liberal veneer. School effectiveness research underwrites, I suggest, a pathological view of public education in the late twentieth century. There is, it appears, a plague on all our schools. Teachers have been infected, school organization has been contaminated and classroom practices have become degenerative and dysfunctional.

In short, schools have become sick institutions. They are a threat to the health of the economic order. Their decline must be countered with potent remedies. Emergency and invasive treatments are called for. Schools need shock therapy administered by outside agencies. Terminal cases merit organ transplants (viz. new heads or governing bodies). And, above all, every school requires targeted INSET therapy. Senior management teams deserve booster steroids to strengthen their macho leadership, while their rank and file colleagues receive regular appraisal-administered HRT (human resource technology) to attenuate their classroom excesses.

From this last perspective, then, school effectiveness research hankers for prototypes – in the form of magic bullets or smart missiles – that are the high-tech analogues of the lobotomies and hysterectomies of the ninineteenth century. It is no accident that Professor David Reynolds, who co-authored a 'mission statement' on school effectiveness and school improvement in 1990, was moved five years later to caution against quackery: 'we need to avoid peddling simplistic school effectiveness snake oil as a cure-all' (TES, 16 June 1995).

For these reasons, school effectiveness research is technically and morally problematic. Its research findings and associated prescriptions cannot be taken on trust. They are no more than sets of assumptions, claims and propositions. They are arguments to be scutinized, not prescriptions to be swallowed.

Key Characteristics of Effective Schools (Sammons et al., 1995) illustrates these problems. It is a 'review of school effectiveness research' commissioned in 1994 by the Office for Standards in Education (OFSTED). The reviews, based at the International School Effectiveness and Improvement Centre of the London University Institute of Education, saw their task as twofold. First, to summarize 'current knowledge' about school effectiveness. Second, to respond to OFSTED's request for 'an analysis of the key determinants of school effectiveness'.

This task redefinition is noteworthy. The extension of OFSTED's remit – the attention to 'current knowledge' as well as 'key determinants' – suggests that the reviewers were reluctant to focus unilaterally on causality. There was, they imply, a 'need for caution' in interpreting 'findings concerning key determinants'.

The redefinition also suggests that the sponsors and researchers did not share the same view of causality. OFSTED appears to espouse a straightforward, linear model of causality. In linear systems, a straightforward cause leads to a straightforward effect. In non-linear systems the outcome is so sensitive to initial conditions that a minuscule change in the situation at the beginning of the process results in a large difference at the end.

OFSTED assumes that, in cases of straightforward causality, outcomes can be linked directly to inputs. OFSTED believes, in effect, that it is possible to predict the final resting place of a clutch of billiard balls on the basis of the prior cue stroke.

The Institute of Education reviewers, however, shared a more elaborate view of causality. They recognize that schooling cannot be reduced to the dynamics of the billiard table. If several balls are simultaneously impelled by separate cues, the play remains straightforward; but it is much more difficult to distinguish the key determinants. Yet, if it is assumed that schools and classrooms are complex, non-linear, adaptive systems, their behaviour ceases even to be statistically straightforward.

The Institute of Education reviewers carefully acknowledge such problems of prediction. Yet, having voiced a series of caveats, they proceed to dilute or disregard them. The notion of key determinants is abandoned, to be immediately replaced by 'key factors'.

Semantic sleight of hand continues. The key factors are packaged in an 'accessible [i.e. tabular] format'. The preamble to this table denotes them as 'correlates *of* effectiveness', whereas the table itself is headed 'eleven factors *for* effective schools' (emphasis added). Social engineering assumptions are smuggled back into the analysis. The factors, that is, provide a better understanding of possible 'mechanisms' of effectiveness.

Once the factors have been identified, however, their aggregation presents further problems. The tacit OFSTED assumption seems to be that causal factors are independent, universal and additive. The OFSTED reviewers, in return, fully acknowledge that these conditions rarely apply in the multivariate world of education. Yet, as before, they appear disinclined to confront OFSTED's innocent assumptions. First, they aggregate results from different studies conducted at different times in different countries. Secondly, they aggregate factors into a summary table. The aspiration to simplify – in the interests of communication (or packaging and marketing) – becomes self-defeating.

The reviewers run into difficulties because they conflate clarification (achieving 'better understanding') with simplification (the extraction of 'key determinants'). They are careful to identify recurrent problems in school effectiveness research. They report, for instance, that previous reviews had commented that 'there is no consensus yet on just what constitutes an effective school'. And they quote another author to the effect that 'defining the effectiveness of a particular school always requires choice among competing values' and that 'criteria of effectiveness will be the subject of political debate'. Overall, the Institute of Education reviewers seem to accept that current school effectiveness debates are as liable to disagreement as any other area of human endeavour. But they make no effort to insert this caveat into their analysis. Clarification is about the honouring of complexity, not its obfuscation.

The conflation of simplification and clarification is also evident elsewhere in the reviewers' arguments. Effective schools, they suggest, are characterized by 'shared vision and goals' (key factor 2) which, in turn, are contingent upon notions of 'a sense of ownership', 'strong input from staff' and 'reciprocal relationships of support and respect' among pupils and staff.

Elsewhere, however, the London Institute review projects a different model of collegiality. Key factor 1 is 'professional leadership', a characteristic that, among other things, should 'usually' be 'firm and purposeful'. Under this last criterion as a subheading, the reviewers go on to quote an American study which suggested that, 'in the early years of ... an improvement drive', effectiveness is also enhanced by 'vigorous selection and replacement of teachers'. Thus, it seems, school effectiveness depends on two kinds of reciprocity: 'strong' input *from* staff and 'purposeful' output *of* staff. Such reciprocity is clearly asymmetrical. Its elaboration and retention serve a rhetorical purpose in the OFSTED review – as a feel-good fiction.

To conclude: *Key Characteristics of Effective Schools* relates to an ill-defined policy field where, the authors admit, reviews outnumber empirical studies. The search for better understanding, it seems, is repeatedly swamped by the desire for policy prescriptions. Such imbalance arises because, as the reviewers also acknowledge, school effectiveness research suffers from a 'weak theoretical base'. The associated demands of social engineering and human resource management outstrip the capacity of the research community to deliver the necessary technical wisdom.

In these circumstances, research is pulled by the market place rather than steered by axioms and principles. It becomes product-oriented. It is expected to supply prototypes configured, in this case, as a package of 'key characteristics'. Sponsored by powerful quasi-governmental agencies, this package is placed – and generously hyped – on the global cash and carry market for educational products. Bundled with a franchising deal and/or a complementary package of technical support, it is then disseminated around the world (e.g. east of Berlin, south of Rome and north of Euston).

I reject both the suppositions and conclusions of such research. I regard it as an ethnocentric pseudo-science that serves merely to mystify anxious administrators and marginalize classroom practitioners. Its UK manifestations are shaped not so much by inclusive educational values that link democracy, sustainable growth, equal opportunities and social justice but, rather, by a divisive political discipline redolent of performance-based league tables and performance-related funding.

The enduring lessons of the school effectiveness literature are to be found in its caveats, not its cure-alls. The OFSTED review should have given greater attention to the value suppositions as well as to the empirical outcomes of such research; to its diversities as well as its central tendencies; and to its exceptions as well as to its 'common features'. By such means, the more enduring aspiration of the Institute of Education reviewers – a 'better understanding' of schooling – might indeed be obtained.

7 Key characteristics of effective schools: a response to 'Peddling feel-good fictions'

Pam Sammons
Peter Mortimore
Josh Hillman

Introduction

The last issue of *Forum* included David Hamilton's reflections on our recent *Key Characteristics of Effective Schools* research review published jointly in April 1995 by the Institute of Education and the Office for Standards in Education (OFSTED). We welcome the opportunity to comment on Hamilton's article which we consider fails to provide an accurate account of the nature, purpose and conclusions of our review. The tone of the critique, with references to 'social Darwinist eugenic rationale' and accusations of 'ethnocentric pseudo-science', is somewhat intemperate, but we have endeavoured to respond to the issues raised in a constructive fashion.

Background

School effectiveness research commenced 30 years ago largely in response to the pessimistic interpretation of findings by researchers in the US (Coleman et al., 1966; and Jencks et al., 1972) about the possible influence of schooling on students' achievement. In the UK seminal studies were conducted in the late 1970s and mid-1980s (Rutter et al., 1979; Reynolds, 1982; Gray et al., 1983; Mortimore et al., 1988; and

Smith and Tomlinson, 1989). The research base was thus established well before the government's market-driven educational reforms were introduced.

Hamilton claims that school effectiveness research is 'ethnocentric' and unconcerned with democracy, equal opportunities or social justice, which suggests that it ignores the powerful impact of socio-economic factors, gender and race. This is untrue as even a cursory reading of much published work shows. In fact, we and other researchers in the field have highlighted the nature of such influences.[1]

Furthermore, school effectiveness research has led to the development of a methodology for separating and identifying the impact of school from the influences of student background factors such as age, low income, social class, gender and race, and their prior achievement levels at entry to school. These studies demonstrate the vital importance of taking account of differences between schools in their intakes so that any comparisons made are done on a 'like with like' basis, thus highlighting the need for the concept of 'value added'.

Such value-added approaches have provided a powerful critique of the simplistic use of raw league tables to measure school performance. We have consistently demonstrated that such tables cannot provide accurate information about the contribution of the school and are especially misleading in relation to the performance of inner city schools (e.g. Sammons et al., 1993a, 1993b and 1994; Mortimore et al., 1994; and Goldstein and Thomas, 1996).

Acknowledging the powerful impact of intake factors, however, does not mean that schools can exert no influence on pupils' educational outcomes. Our work has consistently revealed the existence of both educationally and statistically significant school effects at both secondary and primary levels. In a detailed study of Inner London comprehensives, for example, the difference between the most and least effective schools was over 12 GCSE points – equivalent to 6 grade Bs instead of 6 grade Ds – for a student of average prior attainment (Sammons et al., 1995a). At the primary level, the differences can be even more striking (Mortimore et al., 1988; and Sammons et al., 1995b). Indeed, although no schools overcame the social class difference in attainment between working- and middle-class pupils, our *School Matters* study revealed that, because they made greater progress over three years, working-class pupils in the most effective schools attained more highly than middle-class pupils in the least effective ones. In terms of further education and life chances, such differences are highly significant – especially for disadvantaged groups.

The key characteristics review

Our review was commissioned by OFSTED to inform its revision of the *Framework for the Inspection of Schools*. It was conducted independently and at no point were we requested to make any alterations to the text. Involving an analysis of over 160 publications, it was intended to summarize current knowledge and was based on studies conducted in a variety of contexts and countries. Unlike Hamilton, we feel it is a strength rather than a weakness to adopt an international perspective; a failure to do so would indeed merit the charge 'ethnocentric'! With respect to Hamilton's billiard ball analogy, although we do not advocate a linear model of causality, neither do we accept his alternative proposition that schools and teaching are too complex for analysis to reveal any patterns or consistencies. Our combined research experience leads us to conclude that the study of such patterns is important,[2] and our review provides strong evidence of the existence of 'common features concerning the processes and characteristics of more effective schools'.

We stressed throughout that the review should not be seen as prescriptive and certainly cannot be viewed as a simplistic recipe for effectiveness. It is regrettable that Hamilton fails to report that the summary table to which he takes exception is introduced by the following paragraph.

> These factors should not be regarded as independent of each other and we draw attention to various links between them which may help to provide a better understanding of possible mechanisms of effectiveness. Whilst our list is not intended to be exhaustive, it provides a summary of relevant research evidence which we hope

will provide a useful background for those concerned with promoting school effectiveness and improvement and the processes of school self-evaluation and review.

It is true that in writing the review we attempted to provide information in a format which would be accessible to non-researchers, but we see this as a positive rather than a negative feature and reject the claim that we conflate clarification with simplification. Of course there are dangers of over-simplification in summarizing research findings, but we believe strongly that research should be made available to practitioners and policy-makers. Such accessibility does not have to be simplistic however. For example, with regard to the centrality of teaching and learning we argue that 'the results of our review do not support the view that any one particular teaching style is more effective than others' and went on to conclude: 'Indeed, in our view, debates about the virtues of one particular teaching style over another are too simplistic and have become sterile. Efficient organization, fitness for purpose, flexibility of approach and intellectual challenge are of greater relevance'.

Democracy and research

Hamilton claims that UK manifestations of school effectiveness research:
are shaped not so much by inclusive educational values that link democracy, sustainable growth, equal opportunities and social justice, but rather, by a divisive political discipline redolent of performance-based league tables and performance-related funding.

We reject this view. We hope our review demonstrates that the field has, and continues to have, a strong focus on equity and, as we have noted, that it provides forceful evidence against the simplistic use of league tables. In fact, we think that school effectiveness methods will provide particularly valuable tools for evaluating the impact of recent policy changes concerning educational markets, school status and admissions policies and the (as yet untested) claims that such changes in themselves will raise standards.

We also contest Hamilton's claim that such research 'underwrites ...

a pathological view of public education in the late twentieth century'. In reality, studies have focused much more on the identification of effective schools and effective practices for raising student achievement than on failure – a trend followed in our review. A more telling criticism would be that we have tended to ignore the less effective spectrum of schools and practices in favour of the more effective! Only recently have studies examined so-called 'failing' schools (Reynolds and Packer, 1992; Gray and Wilcox, 1995; Barber and Dann, 1995; Myers and Goldstein, 1996; and Stoll et al., 1996). As Gray and Wilcox have argued 'the correlates of ineffectiveness have been assumed to be the same. It is by no means clear, however, that they are', and further work is needed in this area.

We are aware that reviewing research to inform policy-makers, practitioners and lay audiences may be regarded as controversial in a climate in which education is often treated as a political football. Nevertheless, as argued recently in the *British Educational Research Association's Research Intelligence*, we believe the virtue of research needs to be vigorously asserted.

> We can mobilize rational argument, empirical evidence, critical debate and creative insights. These are of the essence of democracy ... the social responsibility of researchers ... should be to try to disseminate findings not only to fellow researchers, practitioners and policy-makers but also to the general public ... difficulties in simplifying complex findings and fears of misrepresentation by the press are insufficient grounds for trying to hide in simulated ivory towers.
>
> (February, 1996)

We think that Hamilton's comments about 'mystifying' administrators and 'marginalizing' practitioners are misplaced and there are greater dangers in viewing research as suitable only for an academic élite.

Our claims for *Key Characteristics* remain modest: we hope it provides a useful summary for those interested in the results of three decades of school effectiveness research. So far the reactions we have received from practitioners to the review have been overwhelmingly positive. Of course, the findings must not be seen as a panacea and we strongly caution against prescriptive interpretations. However, we hope they will stimulate debate and encourage heads and teachers in the process of evaluating their institutions. We are committed to playing our part in improving understanding of the processes of schooling and we believe that the school effectiveness tradition can make a valuable contribution to this aim.

Notes

1. See, for example, Mortimore et al. (1987a,1987b and 1987c) or Gray et al. (1990).
2. See Mortimore (1995), Sammons et al. (1995b) and National Commission on Education (1996).

8 Beyond school effectiveness and school improvement: lighting the slow fuse of possibility

Michael Fielding

Introduction

The main thrust of the argument I wish to pursue in this paper is to suggest that school effectiveness is importantly flawed and that school improvement conceived as a much more complex, contested process has much to offer, particularly through recent work on the mapping of change. However, I also wish to argue that, like school effectiveness, school improvement stands in need of radical rethinking.

The immediate context of the paper is the work of a group of colleagues, initially based at the University of Cambridge Institute of Education, who over the past six years have developed a particular approach to school improvement called IQEA (Improving the Quality of Education for All). (See Ainscow et al., 1994; Hopkins et al., 1994; and Hopkins et al., 1996.) One of our concerns has been to develop teacher-friendly means of understanding and describing (or mapping) the process of change in ways which are sensitive and sophisticated enough to capture the fine-grained realities and complexities of that process, and in so doing contribute to school improvement.

The first half of the paper (sections 1-3) begins by expressing a number of dissatisfactions with the school effectiveness movement as a prelude to exploring the positive nature and potential of mapping in the school improvement process. The second half (sections 4–5) articulates a number of reservations about both school effectiveness and school improvement and begins to explore the possibility of an alternative, namely 'transformative education', which begins to develop a different framework and set of priorities. My hope is that there is something in this alternative that stretches our imagination and rekindles our enthusiasm for education in times which are too often characterized by the confused, dull and superficial clarity of a severely instrumental schooling. Aware that it is only a start and that it is not the only start, its aspirations seek to draw strength from the truth of Emily Dickinson's saying that 'imagination lights the slow fuse of possibility'.

Why mapping?

Before describing the application of a newly-developed set of research techniques in the context of our IQEA school improvement work, I begin by setting out what seem to me to be important negative aspects of the dominance of the UK national scene by those working in the area of school effectiveness. This underscores the need for methods of investigation which go beneath the surface and help those involved in both the research process and the complex, contested realities of daily life in schools to come to a more adequate understanding of present realities and future possibilities.

The need to challenge the hegemony of school effectiveness

In the UK school effectiveness research[1] is in dire need of challenge. First, because it seems that much of the emancipatory power of its work has been largely distorted – in a national context of surveillance and blame, its potential commitments to equity are virtually negated. Second, because its ascendancy has led to the neglect of important issues to which it is ill-equipped to respond. Much of the school effectiveness work is susceptible to charges of intellectual overheating, an ambivalent relationship to the reality of daily practice and the occupation of a political site which is, by turns, naive or opportunistic and, at worst, complicit in a divisive model of schooling.

With regard to intellectual overheating, a major concern is that, for whatever reason, there seems to be a distressing blindness to the ideologically and epistemologically situated nature of its own intellectual position. Thus, Hamilton argues that the increasingly pervasive influence of school effectiveness research is inversely related to the quality of its heuristic credentials. In his view, school effectiveness research is not only social-Darwinist, but 'an ethnocentric pseudo-science that serves merely to mystify anxious administrators and marginalize classroom practitioners' (Hamilton, 1996: 56, see also p.129, above). For Elliott there is a real question, first, about the platitudinous nature of many of the findings of school effectiveness research, partly because, as White argues above they often amount to little more than empirical illustrations of tautological truths. Second, are not the much-cited factors of school effectiveness research 'the products of an ideological commitment, rather than research, which merely provides a legitimating gloss to mask this fact?' (Elliott, 1996: 207). There is also a third point which comes through strongly from Hamilton's earlier critique (Hamilton, 1994) and is further developed by Elliott. This has to do with the ideological nature of school effectiveness research methodology which is in turn linked to 'an ideology of social control' (Elliott, 1996: 208).

Intellectual overheating does not just manifest itself at the fundamental, paradigmatic level of enquiry; it also emerges at the more specific, intermediate level of debate concerning the conceptual and empirical tools of investigation. A number of examples spring to mind. First, the current preoccupation with increasingly sophisticated measures of added value betrays a myopic understanding of what is meant by an effective school. What is particularly irritating to many critics is not just the substantive point about the valorization of a reductionist notion of schooling, but also the fact that there seems to be a kind of intellectual amnesia at work here. This is especially puzzling given the availability of recent high-quality overviews of school effectiveness research such as that of Silver (1994), which reveals numerous examples of exactly these kinds of criticism being consistently made, both here and in the US, over the last 15 years. A second example, notwithstanding a brief response (Sammons et al., 1996, see above) to Hamilton's recent critique

(Hamilton, 1996), concerns an unacceptably muted awareness of the conflation of causes and correlates, and an equally permissive attitude towards differences between factors and goals (Davies, 1994, see above).

The worry about intellectual overheating is not just its propensity to close down rather than encourage debate. It is that the relative absence of challenge begins to nurture excesses which effectiveness researchers would not themselves approve of, but which their unopposed zeal allows by default. Delight in new possibilities for analysis without sufficient attention given to the appropriateness or adequacy of what is being measured encourages those who think if something cannot be measured then it is not worthwhile and if it is worthwhile then it must be measured. It also tempts others to use a dubious technique rather than wait untill they have a sound one. Warnings from the US are apposite here. Glickman's citation (1991: 8) of remarks by George Hanford, past president of the organization which developed the widely used Scholastic Aptitude Test, is worth reflecting on. Concerned about the excesses and distortions that the use and interpretation of such tests were beginning to produce, Hanford himself warned against creating:

> an aura of precision out of proportion to their significance, which in turn fosters an unsuitable reliance on them, to the exclusion or neglect of other indicators that are equally important and useful.
>
> (Hanford, 1986: 9)

With regard to the ambivalent relationship with the reality of daily practice, the isolation of variables is particularly susceptible to distortions typical of atomistic understandings of the social world which tell us nothing about the interactions, interconnections and contradictions of lived reality (Davies, 1994; and Elliott, 1996). Similarly, the big headings which dominate the lexicon of school effectiveness tend to give a false promise of practical guidance, primarily because they do not take the standpoint of classroom practitioners sufficiently seriously. The confidence and presumption articulated in its modernist tone acts as a de facto denial and dismissal of the historical and the local, of complexity and particularity (Brown et al., 1995; Elliott, 1996; and Perrone, 1989).

If this is to some extent true at institutional level, it is likely to be even more so at the level of classroom practice. My colleagues' suggestion that 'It seems unlikely that the majority of teachers have learned anything of any relevance to the improvement of a single pupil's performance from current school effectiveness research' (West and Hopkins, 1995; see also Brown et al., 1995; Elliott, 1996; Hamilton, 1996; Perrone, 1989; and Riddell et al., 1996) is nearer the mark than many would wish or acknowledge. In similar vein, the preoccupations of the management of effective schools suggest a reality which is too formed in its own likeness to leave sufficient space for doubt about their generalizability to ineffective schools or the possibility that effectiveness is more strongly linked to teacher-related factors (Fitz-Gibbon, 1991).

Concerns about the political naiveté, opportunism and complicity of the school effectiveness movement have recently been eloquently articulated by Elliott who points out that 'As they seek to win friends and exercise influence in the political arena, school effectiveness researchers rarely present their findings as controversial within the educational research community' (Elliott, 1996: 199). Interestingly, he goes on to suggest that this is not just a question of unfortunate omission; rather, it is something closely bound up with processes of intellectual hegemony, 'an attempt to redefine the field of school research in a way which denies the legitimacy of dissenting voices' (Elliott, 1996: 200).

Doubts about the political transparency of school effectiveness research are not, of course, new. One of the major concerns expressed by Lawrence Angus in his review article of a number of key school effectiveness texts concerned their apparent indifference to social and political context (Angus, 1993). Whilst it can be argued that school effectiveness was a necessary corrective to an overly pessimistic, even deterministic, view of the influence of social and political factors on the efficacy of schools, it can equally well be argued in the light of current realities that school effectiveness diverts attention away from structural impediments like poverty and inequality which are conveniently no longer seen as requiring the same degree of imaginative and committed attention from governments, especially those whose political persuasions regard those issues as peripherally important.

Certainly, there is a strong case which points to the politically implicated nature of school effectiveness at a number of different levels. Rather than the putative gold of school effectiveness and government aspirations, the alchemical conjunction with the rise of a market-led model of schooling has produced a narrowing and diminishing of aspirations for both schools and students alike. Thus, recent UK research on academically effective departments in secondary schools (Sammons et al., 1996) suggests academic attainment as problematically related to the creation of confident articulate people.[2] An equivalently destructive myopia has also emerged in the widespread emphasis on GCSE scores that are politically significant in terms of league tables, a preoccupation that effectively serves to marginalize the importance of large numbers of pupils.[3] It is also interesting to observe similar worries across the Atlantic. For example, Glickman argues that:

> the 'effectiveness' movement is unnecessarily restricting the curriculum, narrowing the teaching approach to direct instruction, and controlling teachers by judging them 'on task' only when they teach to specific objectives.
>
> (Glickman, 1987: 624)

Similarly, the market-driven imperative has led to increased internal tension,[4] and a substantial rise in the practice of schools excluding students who do not fit their template of desirable market characteristics or refusing entry to those who seem likely to do so in the future (West and Hopkins, 1995).[5]

This refusal to take the issue of social and political context seriously has a number of other damaging consequences. Among the most commonly encountered is the drift from effectiveness to efficiency (Beare et al., 1989) without any acknowledgement of the differences between the two. Schools can be effective but inefficient, i.e. achieve their objectives, but at too great a cost in terms of value for money. Schools can be efficient but ineffective, i.e. be prudent or parsimonious with regard to resources, but fail to achieve what they would wish. They can also be efficient and effective, but not excellent in a comparative sense.

A further point which is seldom made, but which is equally significant, is that both effectiveness and efficiency are not neutral notions. Whilst this is to some degree seen as acceptable in connection with the notion of effectiveness, that acceptance frequently appears at the margins rather than the centre of debate. Furthermore, what is even less readily acknowledged is the partial nature of efficiency. As Ball (1990) reminds us, a key question is 'efficiency for whom?'. Costs for teachers, such as work intensification, increased surveillance and lack of personal development through work are rarely considered.

Ball's reminder about the non-neutral nature of efficiency underscores a further dimension of the politically implicated nature of school effectiveness. Its preoccupation with 'what works' ignores the question of whose interests shape the nature and process of the work. There is no recognition of the problematic nature of curriculum or of the possibility that schooling may be organized in the interests of, for example, dominant ethnic groups, males or the ruling class (Davies, 1994 above). In fact, there is, perhaps unsurprisingly, no hint of recognition that the research findings of school effectiveness can be seen as 'ideological legitimations of a socially coercive view of schooling' (Elliott, 1996: 200). Nor is there any recognition of the non-educational role of schooling as an agent of social selection.

What is in a fact a deeply political process is masked by an accomplished sleight of hand, which, following Foucault, Dreyfus and Rabinow we can describe as 'political technology' – a process which takes what is essentially a political problem, removes it from the realm of political discourse, recasts it in quasi-technical language and hands it over to specialists in the area (Dreyfus and Rabinow, 1982). This seems to me to have some purchase on the rise and rise of school effectiveness movement: school effectiveness becomes dislocated from considerations about the nature and resourcing of the good life and instead becomes preoccupied with the technical and the measurable within the safe confines of a severely constrained arena of debate.

Central to this process of political technology has been the emergence and proliferation of a peculiarly lifeless, metallic language which has circumscribed and distorted the ways we currently think and act in the

tion (Fielding, 1994; Hall, 1993; and Pring, 1994
nly textured fabric of once familiar educational
d of much of its life, colour and substance.[6]

so worth remarking that the contextual blindness of the
sch   eness movement is itself one of the strongest guarantors
of supp   d furtherance of the political status quo in at least two
respects. First, as Davies points out, it will continue to support the status
quo until research is able systematically to compare schools on a much
wider range of considerations, including such as things as the fostering
of critically and politically aware citizens. In the absence of such
research, the school effectiveness movement will tend to perpetuate the
mythology that if only teachers got a proper professional grip of
themselves, schools could reduce inequality, provide unlimited
opportunity and reverse the decline in national economic competitiveness
for which they are largely responsible (Davies, 1994). Second, and
perhaps more disturbingly, school effectiveness is not merely a supporter
of the political status quo, it is an active agent of its continued
development. School effectiveness is constitutive of a particular view
of social and political reality and is engaged in its further growth and
dominance:

> Effectiveness is a micropolitical vehicle for macropolitical change.
> It is a governmental technology ... Quality and effectiveness are
> not neutral mechanisms. They do not simply improve education,
> they change it. What education is, what it means to be educated are
> changed.
>
> (Ball, 1996)

Methodological context of mapping: developing the hermeneutic response to positivism

In a context such as that previously described, there are good reasons
for welcoming the development and application of a new set of research
techniques (Ainscow et al., 1994) which are not only less cumbersome
and time-consuming than traditional research methods such as interviews,

questionnaires and observations, but also more user-friendly in investigating the complex processes and relationships involved in mapping the process of change in schools.

Six techniques were developed, techniques 1–3 seeking to tap in to the perceptions of individual teachers about the change process and techniques 4–6 the perceptions of the schools as institutions.

Technique 1 – The timeline of change

This technique tracks the relationship between the perceptions of individual staff involved in a change process and the change itself. It is seen as interesting by subjects, not least because it puts the subject firmly in charge of the direction taken by the interviewer and provides a sharp focus for the discussion. The timeline itself, which highlights a number of key events associated with change, provides a short and convenient record of each subject's perception of the change trajectory. By bringing together these differing perspectives, a composite perceived history of the change in the life of the school is established.

Technique 2 – The experience of change

This technique taps the feelings teachers have about specific change. Teachers review a series of 20 cards containing a range of feelings and then select those that best reflect their feelings about the change, which may lead into a fuller discussion or interview. Feelings about change are very difficult to uncover during conventional interviews. This technique legitimates participants talking openly about their feelings, but without forcing any particular words into their mouths. Since the technique takes on average only 15 minutes to complete, it is a very efficient way of capturing hard-to-reach data and makes an excellent companion to the timeline.

Technique 3 – The initiation of change

This technique taps teachers' commitment to change and their sense of control over it. It differs from the previous two techniques in so far as it is concerned with change in general, rather than a specific change. The technique also maps the contrast between changes initiated within and outside of the school. The two sets of five quotations from teachers for both internal and external change are presented, and participants mark the one that most closely accords with their own views. There is also an opportunity for teachers to add a comment of their own. The responses are easy to quantify, and can be rapidly and graphically fed back to groups of staff.

Technique 4 – The culture of school

This technique takes the form of a board game, 'played' in groups of four. Participants privately read the descriptions of four ideal type school cultures. They then make up their own minds which 'culture' their school is closest to, in which direction the school is moving and which is their ideal culture. Teachers commented strongly on how much they enjoyed the board game format and the ensuing discussion with their colleagues. The technique is very efficient in that a single researcher can administer the technique to a whole staff, and give almost instant feedback. A student version of the technique is also available.

Technique 5 – The structures of school

This technique generates data on five of the social structures underlying school cultures: political, micro-political, maintenance, development and service. Participants are presented with two teacher written multi-dimensional cameos for each structure. Each cameo represents one of the two ideal type school cultures, called 'traditional' and 'collegial'. Teachers locate their school on a scale between the two, and are then given the opportunity to describe or comment in writing on their own situation. Finally, teachers suggest an ideal position for their school. By collating the responses, a map of the school's perceived structures and cultures, actual and ideal, is obtained.

Technique 6 – The conditions of school

This technique consists of a scale for measuring a school's internal conditions and capacity for managing change. The 24 items are grouped under 6 conditions: inquiry and reflection, collaborative planning, involvement, staff development, coordination and leadership. The scale can be used as a diagnostic instrument, as a means of measuring a school's progress in creating a development structure, and for comparing the 'change capacity' of different schools. The scale is easy to administer and analyse. It is also amenable to further analysis by subgroup. The technique also complements and cross-validates other techniques in the battery. (Ainscow et al., 1994: 7–8)

It is evident, both from these brief descriptions and from work in the field, that the mapping techniques problematize important areas of school life about which school effectiveness has little or nothing to say. In addition, they:

- are rich in opportunities for individual, small group and communal making of meaning

- acknowledge and seek to articulate the micropolitical, contested nature of school reality

- legitimate and encourage emotional aspects of human experience

- enable the involvement of students in the process of institutional reflection and development.

They help schools to take data from the school effectiveness domain and subject it to the kind of scrutiny that it deserves, but does not always receive.

Thus the common reaction to the apparent underachievement of working-class white males in many UK secondary schools has been either to target that group with additional tutorial support and/or to provide homework clubs and school-based study facilities, without first asking difficult and searching questions about, say, the teacher culture within the school, the relationship between cultures and structures, the problematic nature of the notion of achievement, the counter-productive nature of much homework and so on. Among other things, what these techniques offer is a small, but significant, corrective to some of the dangers of the largely positivist thrust of school effectiveness. They have the potential to problematize the existing framing of the issues, encourage a multifaceted collection of data, and last, but by no means least, to open up – or, as some would have it, 'deprivatize'[7] – the development of a considered response to it.

Integrating mapping into the process of school improvement

By way of illustration of the mapping process itself and its subsequent integration into the process of school improvement, I give the following example which entails the use of a number of the techniques. It involves a comprehensive school catering for 11- to 18-year-old students in a socially deprived urban area.[8] The school has been involved in the IQEA project for a year and a half, during which time it has used three of the six mapping techniques, i.e. T1, T5 and T6.

Putting the results of these together the issues which emerged for consideration were involvement, empowerment, the development of reflective practice, communication and the role of the cadre group (the cadre group being the nine person cross-section of staff, ranging from the headteacher to a classroom teacher in her second year of teaching, who form the developmental, coordinating nucleus of the school's school improvement strategy). With regard to involvement there proved to be a mismatch between low staff scores for parental involvement and very positive staff aspirations and perceptions about parental partnership.

The desire for an empowerment-oriented approach in the school was reflected in the decision to go for a bottom-up model of school improvement mentioned in T1 and in the discussions about the leadership data emerging from the initial administration of T6. The contrast between an empowerment model and the felt reality of its daily operation was also recognized. The challenges and complexities of achieving those aspirations exemplified in the observation 'It is an empowered school, but most of the ideas come from management' became evident in T5.

With regard to reflective practice, discussions arising from T6 emphasized the importance of the school basing its policies on data rather than gut reaction and the companion issue of staff having adequate time to reflect on the data and make sense of it. Discussions also focused on the equally important challenge of supporting the collaborative, even collegial, nature of the process of reflection.

The importance of attending to communication at both a formal and informal level was clearly recognized. Data from both T1 and T6 pointed in particular to the value of staff collectively reminding themselves of the purposes and values that underlay all their efforts in often difficult and unpropitious times.

Finally, the role of the cadre group, which had informed discussion throughout the year, emerged explicitly in the discussion of data from T1. Issues to do with its relation to other staff, its various roles, its own support mechanisms and internal dynamic were identified as important issues.

The overlaying of maps reflecting teacher perceptions of the complexities of change gave the school a richer picture of institutional, departmental and individual realities. A number of action points and strategies emerged, including further professional development days looking at issues to do with the development of reflective practice and the nurturing of a collaborative professional culture, the provision of staff-led workshops and focus groups to service the substantial classroom-focused action-research programme which is at the heart of all IQEA work, small but important changes in organizational structure reflecting an institutional commitment to teachers-as-researchers, the public articulation of a classroom-focused research culture, and the development of critical friendship pairings within the cadre group.

Mapping and its contribution to school improvement

Mapping is a convenient metaphor to apply to the various techniques alluded to in the course of this paper, not only because it conveys the sense of relevant detail and significant features of a school's institutional topography, but also because it links with the recurring companion metaphor of school improvement as a journey. The maps produced with the help of these techniques are perhaps best thought of as heuristic devices to be used and interpreted. They only have meaning as part of a shared undertaking which is itself constantly reassessed and reviewed.

Not only is the journey necessarily an ongoing process, the maps themselves evolve. Their status is always provisional; their perspectives both partial and plural. Mapping is a dynamic process; not only do the maps need re-examining along the journey, they also need to be related to each other and redrawn.

A particular strength of mapping is its capacity to articulate and honour diversity. There is no single technique that is flexible or wide-ranging enough to enable schools to draw a single map which is sufficiently informative. Among the advantages of the six techniques under consideration are:

1. their capacity to produce different but complementary data

2. the propensity of the techniques themselves to encourage and legitimate different styles of learning and give voice to perspectives and possibilities which single or singular approaches capture less effectively.

A further related strength resides in the capacity of mapping to gain access to multiple perspectives and different assumptions. On a number of occasions we have encountered extended dialogue about data finishing with one member of staff saying she did not recognize the school her colleague had been talking about. In some instances, colleagues who share the same perspective discover they believe the same thing, but for very different reasons. In other cases, shared assumptions lead to markedly divergent perspectives. Whilst the fact that teachers' perceptions of the schools in which they work reveal multiple realities is not surprising, the extent and depth of the diversity which was articulated and shared, often amongst those who thought they knew each other well, was striking. It was also testimony to the productive nature of the research instruments and suggestive of their power as agents of communication, not just at the surface level of information exchange, but at the deeper and more significant level of beliefs and values. At this level, staff begin to excavate the nature of the obvious and, hence, the nature of what is potentially both problematic and exciting.

Whilst it would be foolish to suggest that this use of mapping techniques is empowering for those whose voice is seldom heard and too often ignored, they do seem to contain something akin to an aural imperative. Having asked for and received a response to a range of questions directly pertinent to the quality and integrity of school improvement within a particular institution, senior managers cannot respond by asserting the foolishness or error of their colleagues' perceptions. At the very least, they are alerted to issues of poor communication or distorted staff perception. They may respond by acknowledging the existence of a problem and acting appropriately or they may admit they were ignorant of the problem and take steps to find out why. What they cannot do is say, 'Staff are wrong', and carry on as if no-one had been asked a question or provided an answer. False perceptions, whose ever they are and whatever their source, need to be addressed without locating blame.

All this points to the importance of going beyond overly rational approaches to school effectiveness and engaging teachers' perceptions of the realities of classroom and school. We do not know very much about how, say, the findings of school effectiveness research are integrated into the thinking and practice of teachers whose daily work is at the heart of school improvement (Brown et al., 1995). They may not be ready to accept some of the findings. The findings may seem of doubtful relevance to their particular circumstance; they may be seen as trivially true or substantially and irritatingly trivial; they may be seen as having more to do with the political technology of control and blame of teachers than the agency of students' learning. These and a range of other perspectives form an important part of the constrained and contested reality with which school improvement seeks to engage. Unless we develop accessible, realistic methods which help us not only gain access to these perceptions, but also encourage the disposition and drive to engage in dialogue, then school improvement efforts will founder on checklists and league tables which seem to say something with clarity, but too often exclude what is important and tell us less than we thought and more than we understand.

Beyond mapping

From school improvement to transformative education

I have argued so far that the development and use of mapping techniques provides an important contribution to the hermeneutics of school improvement which offers a richer understanding than school effectiveness research of the complex, contested, historically situated reality of schools which then informs our view of the change process.

My conclusion, however, offers a departure from both. It seems to me that if we are to enrich our understanding of how schools might improve, we need to go beyond the largely process-based approaches exemplified in the work of IQEA and ask what view of education we wish to commit ourselves to; in the context of a market-led approach to schooling, the brutality of the invisible hand ensures neutrality is neither possible nor desirable. The same sorts of professional choice which Grace (1995) so helpfully articulates in his study of headship in England seem to me to confront researchers and consultants working in the domain of school improvement. Do we locate ourselves within a framework whose values marginalize education in favour of market-driven economic goals and a severely instrumental, narrowly conceived notion of schooling?

Or do we, as I would advocate, acknowledge the temporary failure of the social democratic project, build on those elements of the postmodern legacy which retain some kind of emancipatory commitment and construct a neomodern (Alexander, 1995) approach to school improvement?

Whilst the articulation and exploration of the theoretical grounding of a neomodernist approach which, following Grace, we might call critical or transformative education studies, is most appropriately dealt with elsewhere, I draw this paper to a close by giving some feel for its intellectual and practical framework by reference to two of examples of what Dale and I have called 'prefigurative' practice (Dale and Fielding, 1989). These focus on two areas:

1.   the development of transformative student involvement

2. the further development of exploratory structures and practices of dialogue which move beyond the residual atomism of collaboration to the potentially transformative mode of collegiality and community (Fielding, 1996a).

The importance of pupil agency – from data source to significant voice

Both in our own work in IQEA and in a number of other approaches to school improvement the importance of involving students in the process of classroom and pastoral monitoring, review and evaluation is widely acknowledged and intermittently practised. Five things separate these transformative proposals from the majority of existing practice:

1. the frequency and pattern

2. the focus

3. the structural articulation

4. the process skills supportive of student involvement

5. most importantly, the purpose of student involvement, the values which provide its rationale and its personal and institutional energy.

First, a transformative approach to student involvement would be one in which the process of involving students was seen as part of the normal way in which a school goes about its daily work. It would be embedded at classroom level, at unit or team level, at intervening institutional level, at the macro level of the school as a learning community and at the interface between school and local, national and international communities (Fielding, 1989).

Second, the involvement goes beyond student comment on aspects of their lives which are seen as safe or without significant impact on the work of adults within the school, and points towards a more wide-ranging, potentially intrusive remit.

Third, transformative student involvement also goes beyond a single teacher's decision to engage in discussions with his or her students to an institutional requirement that those discussions take place on an agreed basis.

Fourth, students are deliberately equipped with both the intellectual and process skills associated with enquiry into the nature of their own and each other's learning and the quality of communal life which they share.

All of these four aspects of student involvement rest upon a fifth. At the heart of the transformational project is a view of education as a key element in the development of a democratic society. Rather than treating students as mere producers of interesting data about the quality of learning and teaching, it regards them as partners in dialogue which informs the life and development of community.

There are, of course, a range of responses to these five aspects of student involvement and there are a number of key issues which remain problematic at both a theoretical and a practical level, e.g. the distinction between 'voice' and 'empowerment' and the further debate about the nature and adequacy of empowerment as an emancipatory imperative (Fielding, 1996c). However, there are a small, but growing, number of instances from both sides of the Atlantic that suggest the potential and the power of a transformative approach involving students. Three examples spring to mind. First, in addition to the now routine involvement of students as an essential source of data about effective teaching and learning, the tentative development within a number of our IQEA schools of involving students in staff tasks groups looking at various aspects of the school's developmental agenda acknowledges the importance of students as agents rather than merely the objects of investigation. Second, in one of our larger secondary comprehensive schools there is a strong commitment to involving students at the very core of next year's teacher research agenda and we are currently exploring a range of ways in which that might break new ground – see Campbell et al. (1994) and SooHoo (1993) in the US. Third, in my own work as a deputy headteacher at Stantonbury Campus, Milton Keynes, one of the UK's pioneer comprehensive schools, we developed a carefully planned partnership scheme between students and staff which enabled us to take forward the integration of students in the decision-making processes of hall meetings (Fielding, 1989).

Developing exploratory contexts for dialogue

The second set of examples concerns the further development of the public realm in schools.

In our IQEA schools there is a commitment, not only to the development of substantial classroom-based, teacher-led research which seeks to understand and change practice in the light of enquiry, but also to a shared process of making meaning. This marks an important shift from what I earlier described as an 'aural' imperative to one which is dialogic. With an aural imperative there is clearly an injunction to listen, but there is no necessary requirement for the data collected to be shared outside a privileged or powerful group; neither is there any requirement that making sense of the data and drawing up possible plans for action be open to all. However, with a dialogic imperative the injunction moves beyond listening to exploring and debating different views and understandings, to the process of making meaning and deciding action together. The locations for that process range from small clusters of teachers, to teams and departments, to the school as a learning community. Examples of this latter whole-school process range from the regular briefing of staff by all departmental research groups, the production of substantial documentation in which each curriculum area seeks to describe both the processes and the conclusions of their research, and in-service days or part-days devoted to the paired running of workshops which explore in interactive ways the fruits of their work in progress. What is also beginning to emerge in some schools is a sense of teachers as members of a research community in which the developing expertise on the nature of teaching and learning, the investigation of pedagogy and the making of meaning, is approached in a collegial rather than a collaborative way.

Despite the fact that this collegial dialogue is of particular importance, with the learning process potentially at its most powerful, it is often skimped or omitted, and teachers are left to make what sense they can of what they encounter. What the transformative perspective would seek to develop here is not just the reporting of teacher research, but the further understanding and nurturing of the way in which both the substance and the process of teachers sharing their work feeds back into the research process itself and, more importantly, the way in which meaning is made.

It is the way that we make meaning together, the emancipatory values that inform that process, and how the whole is linked to action that is central to the transformative perspective. Inevitably, these concerns bring us back to unresolved questions with which teachers and researchers have been grappling for almost two decades – issues such as the nature of teacher cultures, the interdependence of cultures and structures and the distinctions and interrelationships between the atomistic perspectives of individualism and collaboration on the one hand and the communal perspectives of collegiality and community on the other.

Schooling is not enough: only education will do

On the importance of asking different questions

The preoccupations of school effectiveness research currently seem to retain too firm a grip on an instrumental imperative which has too little time to attend to prior questions concerning the nature of education and the good life. They thereby run the risk of exploring with increasing sophistication and dedication areas of contemporary life in schools which gain little purchase on anything other than the transitory, the politically expedient or the coincidentally worthwhile.

School improvement as currently practised in the UK[9] is too closely linked to the school effectiveness project. Despite protestations to the contrary, it is too naive in its process preoccupations and too timid in its attempts to articulate an alternative framework of educational endeavour. Its language is typically and disappointingly as dull and lifeless as that of its effectiveness counterpart and, despite frequent reference to the secular trinity of vision, mission and values, both school effectiveness and school improvement remain for many uninspiring (Perrone, 1989), bland (Riddell et al., 1996) and strangely disconnected from the lived concerns of those for whom education matters even more than schooling (Elliott,1996).

One way of attending to these limitations is to move us on from school improvement to what I have hesitantly called the standpoint of transformative education, a perspective that is different from school improvement in at least three fundamental respects. First, its concerns are explicitly to do with education, rather than just the more limited and derivative notion of schooling. Second, in contrast to the apparent neutrality of the predominantly process-based approach of school improvement, its values are explicit, contestable and contested. Third, its discourse reflects its emancipatory educational commitments and seeks to both reclaim and develop a language which rejects the reductionist commodification of education which blights so much of the national debate in the UK. In sum, it is fundamentally about the development of people as persons in and through community.

This transformative tradition enables us to ask questions which the school effectiveness movement is too preoccupied to notice and the school improvement movement too reluctant to pose, lest it be seen as prescriptive or partial. Yet these are questions which go to the heart of our contemporary dilemmas.

Specific examples focusing round, say, the development of 'value-added' referred to earlier in the paper might include the following: Is the view of value-added one which reflects a commodified view of schooling or one which is more inclusive of wider notions of education? Do the changes in school structures to accommodate value added reflect the imperatives of a 'value-added factory' or are they expressive of a commitment to the development of students as persons?[10] Are the conversations with students focused around an instrumental agenda drawn up by the teacher to serve short-term school goals that have their real origin in the market place or are the conversations occasions for genuine dialogue in which the student's voice speaks of concerns, passions, anxieties and interests which are rooted in his or her developing sense of self? (See Bonnett, 1996.) Do we as teachers, parents, students or members of the community go along with what seems to be an apparently widely held consensus or do we risk uncomfortable questions in the shadow of local and national league tables?

At a general level, such questions are basically about developing the communal architecture of personal and civic courage. As such, they might include the following.

- How do we develop the personal, professional and pedagogic courage to ask hard questions about the nature of education and schooling in an unjust society?
- How can we develop the institutional structures and cultures to enable us to ask those and other questions, listen with our being and make meaning together in ways which are transformative of the human spirit?
- How are we to act with indignation and dignity, with passion and prudence, together and alone, in ways which speak of small integrities in a large world?

Schooling is not enough – only education will do

In closing this paper, it is important to acknowledge that the school effectiveness and school improvement movements within the UK have both helped us to understand a little more about the nature of schooling within a particular social and political context. That understanding is potentially useful and can undoubtedly be utilized in ways which help us to come closer to realizing what we might wish for our children in increasingly uncertain times. However, that context provides severe limits to the developmental possibilities for those working within the school effectiveness domain. Whilst it is less of a constraint for those within the companion domain of school improvement, it nonetheless draws boundaries which its purely process commitments prevent it from breaching. My own view is that a third domain – that of transformative education – deserves serious consideration from those for whom our current circumstances and proposed futures seem bleak in reality and little better in prospect. That approach is characteristically informed by democratic values, dispositions and processes that have at their heart a sense of personhood and human flourishing which is both the purpose of the good life and the means of achieving it. Schooling is not enough; only education will do.[11]

Notes

1. It is important to emphasize that my concerns about what I refer to as 'the school effectiveness movement' are not concerns about the academic integrity or ability of researchers in the field. There are, as in the normal course of debate, aspects of their work with which I naturally take issue. However, I have a number of additional worries which centre round ways in which their research is used to further an educational project which is potentially more damaging than enabling, and a political project which is both pernicious and anachronistic. Intellectual lacuna and political preferment sometimes interact to the detriment of both parties involved; a destructive or diminishing political context has a tendency to highlight the worst rather than the best of those whose work is looked on with particular favour.

2. Particularly pertinent here is Glickman's observation: 'In my opinion, teaching for specific academic achievement has much to commend it. But the question remains, At what expense?' (Glickman, 1987: 624).

3. The counter-suggestion that a significant improvement in GCSE passes gives the lie to this claim illustrates my point nicely. My concern is that many schools have become overly, if understandably, preoccupied with GCSE pass rates – usually around the C/D grade level – and one of the consequences of that preoccupation has been first, the relative neglect of students who are likely to get grades below D and, second, a marginalization of aspects and expressions of education which have to do with education not captured by external examinations of this kind. In these and other senses, the market has narrowed and diminished the aspirations of both schools and students and is likely to continue to do so.

4. Teachers and researchers who spend time in schools will, I suspect, recognize the picture to which I am alluding, one in which there is significantly more friction and balkanization as a result of internal league tables. A recent illustration from my own experience came from a participant in a national assessment coordinators' network who observed that whilst school effectiveness research had appropriately made it more problematic to blame students or their communities for educational underachievement, the current circumstance had resulted in teachers blaming each other.

5. Rises in exclusion rates and the new impetus to select pupils fostered by recent government legislation are part of current debate. The comments of a Coventry head of mathematics cited in a recent article by Jones illustrate these dilemmas well:
    The league tables are the most destructive piece of legislation. Instead of getting the best education for each child it becomes a question of what a child can contribute to the school's league table. Are they a problem or an asset? This is a downward spiral (Jones, 1996: 13).

6. My intention is not to paint an unrealistic or nostalgic picture of life before 1988. Rather it is to draw attention to the power of discourse to change the way we think and act. It is also to suggest that the technicist turn which Elliott (1996) describes so convincingly has linguist manifestations which both reflect and further its ambitions.

7. The term comes from the work of Louis and Marks (1995).

8. For a more detailed account of this example, see Fielding (1995).

9. It is interesting to note that there is a very different picture in the US, where there are a number of approaches to school improvement that go well beyond largely process considerations to embrace a particular set of values and a particular view of schooling and education. An example which is explicitly concerned with the furtherance of a democratic project can be found in the work of Glickmann (1993).

10. Contrast the kind of thin instrumentalism I am alluding to here with the richness and fullness of the person-centred approaches to dialogue with students described in *Teaching for Democracy* (Wood, 1990).

11. This paper is a shortened and revised version of my 1996 AERA paper (Fielding, 1996b). My acknowledgements and thanks remain virtually the same. Firstly, my thanks to Mel West, whose intellectual energy and irreverence have been the source of a number of these ideas and, in disagreeing with him, the stimulus to others. Special thanks to a number of other colleagues and friends who gave me both moral support and intellectual challenge in the final stages of the writing of this paper. They include Stephen Ball, Michael Barber, Michael Bonnett, Wilf Carr, Donald McIntyre, Mary James, Ben Levin, Richard Pring, Geoff Southworth, John White and Patricia White. Thank you, too, on these counts and also for his patience and commitment to the work of IQEA, to our research assistant John Beresford. Thanks, in particular, to David Hargreaves, whose disagreements are always so demanding, so stimulating and so passionately infused with intellectual and moral courage. Finally, reiterated thanks to John White for his encouragement and patience and for his admirable persistence and steadfastness of purpose in bringing together this collection of papers.

9 The missing hermeneutical dimension in mathematical modelling of school effectiveness

David Scott

School effectiveness researchers (Creemens and Scheerens, 1989; Levine, 1992; and Mortimore et al. 1988) have in recent years made a number of claims about education systems. Their thesis is that individual schools make a difference to the relative achievements of children regardless of the socio-economic conditions in which those schools operate. For example, Smith and Tomlinson (1989: 301) argue that there are very important differences between urban comprehensive schools in terms of the progress made by their pupils: the findings show that the same child would get a CSE grade 3 in English at one school, but an O Level grade B in English at another.

There are equally large differences in maths and in exam results in total across all subjects. They employ a methodology which involves the application of mathematical models to various complicated social processes. This allows them to separate out the effects of a number of variables which it is thought have an impact and to calculate the residual. This is defined as the school effectiveness quotient or that which is added by the school as a result of teaching and learning processes. Mortimore (1992: 32) argues that we define an effective school broadly as one in which students progress further than might be expected from consideration of its intake – pupils are only being effectively taught if their achievements go beyond what would normally be expected of them.

This mathematical modelling of schooling measures performance in a standardized way – to allow comparisons between individual pupils in different settings. Furthermore, modellers choose those attributes which can be more easily quantified (i.e. reading ages as they are measured on a standardized test) or which have already been quantified (i.e. GCSE, Key Stage test or A Level scores). Researchers in this field, therefore, take up a value position from the outset and this contributes to their definition of effectiveness. Methodological requirements influence the construction of their conceptual schemata and epistemological frameworks.

Performance is emphasized and this is performance of a kind which can be reliably quantified.

However, these measurements refer to performance at a certain point in time and in controlled conditions and not to the levels of competence reached by the child. Wood and Power (1987) distinguish between performance and competence (see Table 1) and develop this distinction along two axes. The first relates to performance in the test situation – whether the child is successful or unsuccessful at the task. The second axis refers to what the child can do.

Thus two types of errors may result – false negative and false positive – and these occur because of the gap between competence and performance.

Table 1 Error types in relating performance to competence

	Success on task	*Failure on task*
Child has underlying competence (in sufficient degree)	Performance correlated with competence	False negative error – failure due to factor other than lack of competence
Child does not have underlying competence (in sufficient degree)	False positive error – success due to factor other than competence	Performance correlated with competence

This can be illustrated by reference to recent evidence regarding the improvement in the performance of girls at GCSE and A Level in relation to the performance of boys (see Elwood, 1996). One possible explanation is that since the examination technology was changed (i.e. by the introduction of coursework in the GCSE and to some extent at A Level), girls are now better able to express what they can do, though Elwood (1996: 300) suggests that this is not 'the sole explanatory factor'. In the past, therefore, girls' underachievements related in part to the way they performed in test situations (i.e. as a result of the test technology) and not to their general levels of competence. However, it is impossible to separate out these two in any meaningful way. This is so for two reasons:

1. the level of performance achieved by children influences what and how they learn and, therefore, affects the competence levels they achieve at a later point in time

2. the gap between competence and performance for individual children varies and cannot be measured.

If it is suggested that a more accurate (that is better expression of competence) could be obtained by repeated testing and repeated measurement, this can not solve the problem, since for some children it is those factors which inhere in the testing process itself that sustain the gap between performance and competence. False negative errors in testing make reference to an ideal which can be inferred but not quantified. If it could then it would be possible to argue that, with a more sophisticated testing technology, the gap between competence and performance could be eliminated. We could then be certain that a child's performance accurately reflects what she is able to do. Hammersley (1992) distinguishes between different meanings of the word 'accuracy' when he argues that precision or accuracy may not be best expressed quantitatively.

Accurate descriptions of phenomena depend on their relation to the objects to which they refer and not to their ability to be expressed in mathematical form.

It is possible to go beyond this and suggest that the distinction between competence and performance referred to previously implies a particular way of understanding this relationship and is, therefore, a theory-laden concept. Vygotsky (1978) argues that a more useful notion of performance does not refer to the ability of the child to operate in standardized conditions, but to the ability of that child to perform in conditions that maximize performance. This, of course, might include collaboration between child and adult/teacher/tester. This refers to the zone of proximal development: competence is here being defined as the capability of the child to progress to higher levels of learning. Gipps (1994) characterizes this as a form of educational description and contrasts it with psychometric testing. So it cannot be measured for a number of reasons:

- best rather than typical performances are examined
- it takes place in relatively uncontrolled conditions
- it is essentially ipsative and thus seeks to make comparisons between different performances of the child rather than between performances of different children.

This would suggest that standardized approaches to the collection of data used by school effectiveness researchers imply a theory about assessment and do not simply measure what is.

So one problem which has been identified is that although school effectiveness researchers claim to describe what the school adds on to the learning of the child and that some schools add on more than others because they apply certain pedagogical and organizational principles to the process of schooling, in fact what they are referring to is performance on a narrow range of tests.

Schools may be able to improve performance by the adoption of certain measures, but this does not necessarily relate to learning, i.e. to what the child is able to do. Indeed, a school might be adept at improving performance, i.e. the ability to take a test, without being skilled at consolidating and accelerating learning. If it is argued that each pupil in each school has an equal chance of performing well and that, therefore, even if we cannot measure competence, performance reflects competence in a straightforward linear fashion, we have already suggested that this is not so. This is because those factors which mediate between competence and performance are variables which differ between schools, i.e. gender (girls perform better in certain types of testing situations than others) (Gipps and Murphy, 1995).

A second problem with using test scores is different. This is to do with the reliability of the marking of such tests. Nuttall (1995: 57) reminds us that research evidence suggests that the margin of error in a candidate's grade at O Level or CSE is about one grade in every direction.

Again it can be argued that if we compare school with school, each school has the same chance of marking error with regard to their scores and that therefore the comparison is still valid.

However if we are using multilevel modelling techniques as many school effectiveness researchers do (see Goldstein, 1987) with their reliance on data gathered at the individual level and matched pairs of children, this matching becomes suspect.

I have examined one kind of variable and pointed to a number of problems with its identification.

These are of course methodological problems, though undoubtedly they have implications for epistemology: that is, the methods we choose to enable us to understand phenomena in the world impact on the way we conceptualize these phenomena. I now want to examine the other set of variables used by school effectiveness researchers – 'those common features concerning the processes and characteristics of effective schools' (Sammons et al., 1995: 11).

Levine (1992) for example, argues that schools which are unusually effective in value-added terms show the following characteristics:

- productive school climate and culture
- focus on student acquisition of central learning skills
- appropriate monitoring of student progress
- practice-oriented staff development at the school site
- outstanding leadership
- salient parent involvement

- effective instructional arrangements and implementation
- high operationalized expectations and requirements for students.

In a similar manner, Sammons et al. (1995, see above) suggest that the following 11 interdependent factors are significant:

- professional leadership
- shared vision and goals
- an orderly and attractive working environment
- concentration on teaching and learning
- purposeful teaching
- high expectations
- positive reinforcement
- monitoring progress
- pupil rights and responsibilities
- home–school partnership
- school-based staff development.

There is a marked absence of curriculum factors. This de-emphasis of what should be taught in schools separates out curriculum from pedagogic and organizational concerns. A school could be an effective school regardless of what it teaches and what values it inculcates into its pupils. This separation of content from pedagogy is underpinned by a behavioural objectives model of curriculum design and a technical rationalist view of pedagogy. In the first case, schooling is understood as a linear process which starts with the development of clear objectives or goals, proceeds through to the selection of content which is specified in behavioural terms – that is its acquisition must be an observable or testable process – and finishes with the evaluation of that process to see if those objectives have been met. As Tyler puts it:

> if an educational program is to be planned and if efforts for continued improvement are to be made, it is very necessary to have a

conception of the goals that are being aimed at. These educational objectives become the criteria by which materials are selected, content is outlined, instructional procedures are developed and tests and examinations prepared.

(Tyler, 1949: 3)

In the second case, it implies a particular model of teaching behaviour. If research is understood as the development of propositions about educational activities which reflect the world as it is, allow predictions about future educational states, and can be replicated by other educational researchers (see Levine, 1992; and Sammons et al., 1995), then this provides support for the technical-rationality model of the relationship between theory and practice. Here we refer to a model which understands the practitioner as a technician whose role is to implement objective educational truths, and, therefore, as having a passive role in the implementation process. If it is possible to identify such truths about education, the practitioner who chooses to ignore them is likely to make inadequate judgements about he or she they should proceed in practice. This is regardless of the need for practitioners to own or incorporate such findings into their own understandings to inform their practice (Rudduck, 1991). If theory about education can be developed which transcends context, then practice is better informed by it. The epistemological basis of the research methodology adopted and the development of lists of qualities to which educational practitioners are expected to conform reinforces this way of thinking.

This can be contrasted with process-orientated models of curriculum design and deliberative discourses of teacher behaviour (see Walsh, 1993). The behavioural objectives model has been criticized (see Stenhouse, 1975; and Elliott, 1983) for the following reasons.

1. Complex and important learning outcomes of any educational programme may be neglected at the expense of the more trivial and less important, because it is easier to describe them in behavioural objective terms.

2. The prespecification of behavioural goals may encourage an inflexibility of approach within the classroom and learning outcomes

which may incidently flow from classroom interaction will be deliberately underexploited.

3. There is a danger of assuming that if something cannot be measured, then it cannot be assessed and therefore it should not be a part of the learning process.

4. Lists of intended behaviours do not adequately represent the way we learn: this is because logical order cannot be conflated with pedagogic process. As McLaren says, 'Knowledge cannot be theoretically abstracted from its own production as part of a pedagogical encounter' (McLaren, 1995: 41).

Equally, the technical-rationality model has been criticized because it seeks to treat teachers as technicians, whose role is simply to follow sets of pre-ordained specifications. In contrast, the deliberative is defined as those behaviours which lead to wise actions. It is, therefore, concerned with practical theorizing and can only be judged to have succeeded by whether it has contributed to improved practice. However, the point I wish to make is not to debate these various issues, but to suggest that what is seemingly unproblematic is in fact underpinned by a theoretical position, an epistemological stance, a particular understanding of theory and practice, and a conceptualization of the relationship between the two.

In short, different approaches to researching schools will reflect different positions on these important issues (see Carr and Kemmis, 1986; Walsh, 1993; and Scott and Usher, 1996).

Two further issues need to be addressed in relation to these specifications of desirable behaviours.

The first concerns the implicit unilinear model of causation subscribed to by school effectiveness researchers. Educational practice may be conceived of as deliberative action designed to achieve certain ends. What this implies is that there may be a number of different ways which are equally appropriate to achieve those ends. Indeed, educational subjects may respond in different ways to different pedagogic and organizational routines. However, the use of mathematical models to describe educational settings and the production of lists of specified behaviours would suggest a unilinear approach to school effectiveness. Quantitative modelling necessarily leads to certain ways of understanding schools and precludes others.

The second issue concerns the relationship between correlations and causal mechanisms. Even if a correlation can be established between two variables, it is still not possible to assert that the one caused the other to happen in an unproblematic way. There is always the possibility of a third variable causing variance in both. Furthermore, we cannot be sure as to which variable is prior to the other. Sanday (1990), for example, examines the first finding of a study by Mortimore et al. (1988) into effectiveness criteria in primary schools. He asks the following three questions.

1. Does the observed correlation between the effective school (as it is identified by a battery of achievement tests conducted on its pupils) and purposeful leadership by the headteacher indicate that an effective school has to have this characteristic?

2. Can a school function effectively without such leadership?

3. Even if the headteacher does show purposeful leadership, could the school still be ineffective?

Correlations are literally no more than this and need to be distinguished from causal relationships.

Bhaskar (1979) makes a distinction between epistemology and ontology, in which he argues that epistemology is always transitive and, therefore, by definition as much a product of prevailing power arrangements in society, but that ontology – certainly with regards to the human sciences – is relatively enduring and thus has a degree of intransitivity about it. Bhaskar needs to make this distinction to sustain his attack on positivism and its insistence on the atheoretical nature of data, and to cement in place his version of transcendental realism, which can be characterized in four ways:

1. there are objective truths whether they are known or not

2. knowledge is fallible because any claim to knowledge may be open to refutation

3. there are transphenomenalist truths in which we may only have knowledge of what appears and this refers to underlying structures which are not easily apprehendable

4. most importantly, there are counter-phenomenalist truths in which those deep structures may actually contradict or be in conflict with their appearances.

We have already suggested that regularities between phenomena which produce correlations cannot in themselves uncover causes. If we make the assumption that they can, then we fall victim to what Bhaskar (1979) described as the ontic fallacy, the unjustified conflation of the epistemological and ontological realms. We can see this most obviously in some well-known examples. A hooter in London signalling the end of the day's work in a factory does not cause workers in Birmingham to pack up and go home, even if the two phenomena correlate perfectly over a period of time. A good correlation has been discovered between the human birth rate and the number of storks in different regions of Sweden, but the one does not cause the other to happen. The reason why these do not show causal relations and can, therefore, be described as spurious correlations is because the regularities so produced do not relate in a straightforward manner to the causal mechanism which produced them. One of the reasons for this is, as Bhaskar argues, that deep structures may actually have contradictory appearances. But more importantly, the way they have been expressed, i.e. in mathematical form, is an inappropriate way to describe them. Mathematics is an acausal system and can give us indications of causal relationships but never exact descriptions. However, ironically, the very precision demanded by the use of quantitative methods acts as a smokescreen to our determining whether our descriptions of causal mechanisms are accurate or inaccurate.

If the causal mechanism (this is an ontological matter) which we are trying to describe is to be perfectly aligned with the regularities we observe (and this is an epistemological matter), then we have a closed system. Science has been so successful because it has either created closed systems (i.e. much chemical/physical research) or been able to operate in closed systems (i.e. astronomy).

For a closed system to operate we have to be certain of two conditions. First, that the mechanism itself remains coherent and consistently so, i.e. that there is no change in the object over a period of time or across cases. Bhaskar calls this the intrinsic condition for closure. Second, that the relationship between the causal mechanism and those external conditions which allow it to operate remain constant. If teachers in a school come to believe that democratic forms of management are inappropriate, then the effectiveness of those forms of management are likely to decline. The external conditions for the effectiveness of democratic systems have changed because one of them was a belief in democracy, and thus the system can no longer be thought of and treated as a closed system.

What are the implications of this? The most important one is that we cannot make predictions about future states with any degree of conviction from open systems. This is so because of the double hermeneutic involved in all social research. Human beings both generate and are, in turn, influenced by social scientific descriptions of social processes. As Giddens argues, this introduces an instability into social research which immediately renders data and those findings produced by methods appropriate to the discovery of closed system truths problematic:

> The Social Sciences operate within a double hermeneutic involving two way ties with the actions and institutions of those they study. Sociological observers depend upon lay concepts to generate accurate descriptions of social processes; and agents regularly appropriate themes and concepts of social science within their behaviour, thus potentially changing its character. This ... inevitably takes it some distance from the cumulative and uncontested model that naturalistically-inclined sociologists have in mind.
>
> (Giddens, 1984: 31)

There is though a second and more fundamental sense given to the notion of the double hermeneutic. Human beings, as reflexive and intentional actors, are engaged in interpretive activity throughout their lives. Symbolic interactionists argue that it takes a particular form: social actors come to see the world as others see it and to see the world as others see them. They are thus able to reflect on, and reflexively monitor, their own actions. However, the presence of the researcher and the researcher's desire to investigate social reality by focusing on the perceptions and behaviours of social actors requires a further level of interpretation. The double hermeneutic involved in this determines the types of closure that we can make when we describe social reality.

However, mathematical modellers of school processes attempt to create closed systems of a different kind. The attempt at quantification always involves a series of reductive moves during the research process. Here we need to introduce the idea of two competing systems of thought.

The first is the extensional idiom and this is the system which is used by mathematicians. Standard logic attends only to matters of literal truth or falseness: it is concerned only with the statement's extension. What this implies is that scientific description cannot concern itself with the intentions, beliefs, propositional attitudes of social actors – in short, that the intentional idiom is illegitimate.

This belief, and this would point to its self-refuting character (Wilson, 1990), has underpinned mathematical, physical and chemical science research programmes and, indeed, much work in behaviourism, sociobiology and psychology. However, if we accept that social actors are conceptually different from inanimate objects, this creates certain problems in the application of mathematical models. As Wilson points out:

> it is crucially important here to note explicitly that use of a mathematical model does not imply that descriptions are untainted by intention. Rather when we develop and apply such a model we arrange to package intentional idioms in such a way that, for the purpose at hand, we can proceed with formal calculations.
>
> (Wilson, 1990: 398–9)

We can do this in a number of ways and, in doing so, we always proceed using the principles of additivity, linearity and proportional variation, and we make the assumption that objects to be compared over time (and the time factor is crucial when we are dealing with regularities) are invariant in their properties. Otherwise we are measuring different phenomena. If, on the other hand, the logic of the intensional idiom is that human activity is context dependent, then it is harder for us to be certain that we are comparing like with like. That is, as Wilson (1990) points out, we make certain compromises with the data as soon as we use methods whose sole purpose is to allow us to quantify. These compromises involve the use of deductive techniques (as in much experimental work), the use of pre-set instruments (i.e. likert scales in questionnaires) which determine and frame the types of answers we get as researchers and the use of statistical techniques to analyse the data.

It is not that the types of closure occasioned by these techniques and by the use of these instruments are not paralleled in qualitative research, but the problem is that these forms of closure are determined beforehand to allow the development of mathematical models and, therefore, do not allow actors' descriptions of social life ever to be faithfully reflected in our research accounts. Indeed, the hermeneutical circle (see Gadamer, 1975) can in a sense never be completed and thus always involves a break of one sort or another. But more importantly, as Giddens (1984) argues, the production of models has to proceed from descriptions of social life by the actors involved and we have to do everything we can to allow social actors to deliver to us authentic accounts of their lives.

It has been argued that, if the researcher wants to investigate structural arrangements in society, then survey methods are usually considered to be the most appropriate. If that same researcher now wants to investigate a cultural setting, then he or she is more likely to use ethnographic methods. However, this gives a false picture. Giddens (1984), for example, suggests that social structures only have substance, and then only fleetingly, in the reasons agents have for their behaviours. He is, therefore, arguing that data which refer to the knowledgeability of agents are essential elements in social research, whether such study is of a macro-, meso- or micro-type. Methods which prevent the researcher from gathering reliable and valid data about this are not, therefore, appropriate or useful.

Giddens (1984) further elucidates four levels of social research. The first is the hermeneutic elucidation of the frame of meaning of the social actor(s) involved. The second is the investigation of context and the form of practical consciousness. The third is the identification of the bounds of knowledgeability and the fourth is the specification of institutional orders. His argument is that quantitative researchers either pay insufficient attention to the first, collect data about it in the wrong order or ignore it altogether. What this schema also implies is that a purely phenomenological perspective is inadequate. This is so for four reasons:

1. social actors operate within unacknowledged conditions, that is, societal structures in which the actor is positioned

2. there are unintended consequences of his or her actions

3. social actors operate through tacit knowledge which is hidden by virtue of what it is, or at least cannot and is not articulated during the formation of explanations of action

4. the social actor may be influenced by unconscious motivation.

What this points to is the inevitable objectification involved in social research (that is the going beyond the purely phenomenological perspective) (see Bhaskar, 1989).

However, as Giddens argues, this going beyond, in order for the explanation to be valid, has to involve an understanding of the perspectives of social actors and the implications of this is that methods have to be appropriated which do not distort those meanings. There is, therefore, always an ethnographic moment in social research and this cannot legitimately be written out by quantitative researchers.

The missing hermeneutical dimension in mathematical modelling of school effectiveness has the following two consequences.

1. A full and accurate account of what happens in schools (the descriptive element) and of how we can improve them (the normative element) is not available.

2. Since the theoretical presuppositions of this type of research are not made explicit, it is difficult for us to make a judgement about the political and ethical agendas which underpin it. Research, in short, always needs to be reflexively adequate.

10 Endpiece: a welcome and a riposte to critics

Peter Mortimore
Pam Sammons

Introduction

Research in the social sciences is frequently difficult to undertake. Parents and children tend not to live in towns or to attend schools in patterns that fit easily with research designs. The reality of uneven, overlapping, mixed contexts and subjects provide researchers with considerable methodological challenges and – for those working with quantitative methodologies – the need for statistical techniques that can cope with such complexity.

Because social and educational research is difficult, there is a tendency to see criticism as unfair or inappropriate. This is wrong. Of course some critics will be fired by ideological fervour and some will be ignorant of the work that they seek to criticize, but others will be motivated simply by a healthy desire to challenge accepted findings. We believe that research in education and the other social sciences develops and improves through critical review and through the challenge and refutation of both findings and theories. That said, we – and surely researchers in general – expect criticism of our work to be undertaken seriously, reported evenhandedly and presented in a way which avoids personal attacks.

It is surely only fair that those who seek to criticize should first have studied the major works in the field in detail. It is not good enough to cite secondary sources, nor is it good scholarship simply to make serious allegations without presenting supporting evidence. At the Institute of Education we have sought to develop a reasoned approach to a critique which focuses on the methodology of the research in question and, whilst it may challenge its conclusions, endeavours to avoid personal attacks on the author. This is the approach which some of us at the Institute tried to adopt when we published a critique of some recent OFSTED research (Mortimore and Goldstein, 1996). This approach, however, did not save us from an emotional and vituperative riposte by a journalist in a national newspaper (Phillips, 1996).

School effectiveness provokes criticism from all quarters: our research peers, politicians of all parties and, most recently, from the head of OFSTED (Woodhead, 1997). We are grateful to the editor for the opportunity to reply to those critics who have contributed to these papers, but we obviously cannot answer on behalf of the many researchers (in this country and elsewhere) who have written about this field of enquiry. We will respond, therefore, drawing – where this seems appropriate – on our own research studies carried out over the last 20 or so years. We are pleased to note, however, that school effectiveness research has also been welcomed by both practitioners and academics.

We will not attempt to respond to every critical comment that has been made in any of the papers. We have discussed many of the general issues over the years (Mortimore et al., 1988a, 1988b and 1988c; Mortimore, 1991a; Mortimore, 1995a; Sammons et al., 1993a) and some similar points have already been answered in the autumn edition of *Forum* (Sammons et al., 1996a) and in the *Cambridge Journal of Education* (Sammons and Reynolds, forthcoming). Furthermore, we will not address a number of technical points (such as Winch's query as to whether it is possible to calculate residuals based on pupil-level data or on the importance of taking into account the number of pupils involved in any analysis). These have been addressed in detail in Goldstein's recent publication on the limitations of league tables (Goldstein and Speigelhalter, 1996).

Instead, we have selected the key generalizable issues and will endeavour to deal with these. We are sure that this will not resolve all the concerns that have been raised and we welcome continued dialogue on what we deem to be an important area of research.

Definitions of effectiveness

A number of the contributors to these papers challenge the very concept of 'effectiveness'. Some, like White, see it as unnecessary. For him it is simply a matter of ends and means. Our view, which we have consistently applied to our research over the years, is that some operational definition of effectiveness is necessary for empirical research. Accordingly, we have tried to set the achievement of pupils within the context of the capacity of the school to promote progress. This is because we recognize that schools do not receive uniform intakes of pupils. Some schools take those who come with high levels of prior achievement or with considerable social advantage, whilst others predominantly receive pupils who lack these benefits. We have sought to find ways to distinguish the impact of the school from the dowry brought by the pupil. One definition we have used is that an effective school is 'a school in which students progress further than might be expected from a consideration of its intake' (Mortimore, 1991b).

This definition is built on the premise that an expectation for any particular school intake group can be calculated on the basis of the average levels of achievement recorded by pupils with different background characteristics in a population or a large sample of schools. More effective schools are those which exceed this expectation. Less effective ones are those where pupils do less well than expected on the basis of their given characteristics. Scott, in his criticism of the definition, slips from our focus on the school to the teaching and claims that we argue, 'pupils are only being effectively taught if their achievements go beyond what would normally be expected of them'. This is a subtle change, but an important one, which distorts our argument.

Two assumptions lie at the heart of the definition: that any pupil's outcome in a given performance test will be related to both his or her individual characteristics and background and to the quality of their total school experience, including the teaching the pupil has received; and that those schools in which pupils systematically perform markedly better than the average for the whole population of the schools – once the individual characteristics and background differences have been taken into account – are *prima facie* likely to be better than the others. We term such schools effective. They may receive pupils who are exceptionally talented or very ordinary. The pupils may have done well or badly in previous educational settings. Nevertheless, these differences should not by themselves affect the effectiveness or otherwise of the school.

The definition we have quoted is still used quite widely, although it has been elaborated in a number of cases (e.g. Stoll and Fink, 1996). Sam Stringfield and David Reynolds have adopted a commercial concept and used the phrase 'high reliability organizations' to illustrate their view of effective schools (Reynolds, 1995).

A different type of definition which we have sometimes used attempts to deal more explicitly with the impact of family background:

> an effective school regularly promotes the highest academic and other achievement for the maximum number of its students, regardless of the socio-economic backgrounds of their families.
>
> (Mortimore, 1996a)

These definitions share similarities. They focus on the capability of the school to make a difference. They can also cope with the reality that the playing field for pupils' performance is seldom level and that progress for some pupils – and for some schools – will be harder than for others.

The concept of effectiveness is not simple, but it provides a way of describing schools which is not dependent on either their intake or their outcomes alone, but on the relationship between both.

Methodology of effectiveness

The concept of effectiveness depends on the ability of researchers to integrate data on the intake characteristics of pupils and data on their outcomes. Both are important and any choice of variables is bound to be open to debate. We have tended to use prior achievement at the end of a previous phase of schooling as our favoured intake variable and have fine-tuned its effects with information on pupils' background characteristics and – if appropriate – with the contextual effects made up of the aggregated impact of individual characteristics (Mortimore et al., 1988a and 1988b; Gray et al., 1990; Goldstein et al., 1993; Sammons et al., 1993a; Sammons et al., 1994; and Thomas and Mortimore, 1996).

Twenty years ago, our earlier studies had to make use of rudimentary standardization procedures but, in recent times, the development of multilevel modelling (MLM) able to take account of the nested nature of educational data has made the process much more reliable when large samples are available (Paterson and Goldstein, 1991). MLM represents a way in which valid and reliable judgements can be made about particular sets of results. In particular – and in marked contrast to the use of crude league tables – it demonstrates that a relatively small number of schools can be distinguished with significantly better or worse results than others at any particular time or, if results are available, over a period of years.

White argues that the effectiveness of a school will be self-evident. On the basis of the analysis of hundreds of schools over a number of years (e.g. Thomas and Mortimore, 1996) we disagree. We have concluded that only empirical research is capable of teasing out – in a reliable way – the relationship between the intake and outcomes. Our recent study of secondary school departments has indeed shown quite different levels of effectiveness for different subjects. We found evidence, for example, that in some institutions highly effective and ineffective departments coexisted (Sammons et al., 1996b). As a result of this and other research, we have drawn attention to the need to consider complexities in the judgement of school performance and have highlighted the need to ask the following three key questions:

1. Effectiveness for which outcomes?

2. Effectiveness over which period of time?

3. Effectiveness for whom?

We have thus sought to extend the concept of effectiveness to include the dimensions of consistency, stability and differential effects (Sammons, 1996).

The choice of the outcomes

A number of critics raise the point that school effectiveness researchers have focused exclusively on a limited range of academic outcomes. Scott goes further and raises the distinction, drawn from studies of language, between competence and performance. We accept that we have not attempted in any of our work to diagnose the underlying competence of pupils. How could anyone have done so? On the other hand, we have collected and used a much broader range of outcomes than most critics acknowledge and we intend to use more. We have used, in addition to reading and mathematics tests, practical mathematics tasks, speaking assessments and writing assignments as well as measures of self-concept, attitude to school, attendance and behaviour (Mortimore et al., 1988a and 1988b) and are currently engaged in a large-scale study in Scotland with the University of Strathclyde, in which we are collecting a number of potential attitudinal outcomes (Robertson et al., 1996).

Of course, the outcomes which we have adopted cannot encompass the whole of a child's development. It is true that, as Winch notes, we have largely ignored the individual aims of schools. This is because we found, in *Fifteen Thousand Hours* (Rutter et al., 1979) and *School Matters* (Mortimore et al., 1988) that the amount of variation between the aims that schools articulated was, in fact, relatively small.

We must respond to the comments in some of the articles that the academic outcomes that we have used are not desired by parents. Of course parents want schools to give their children other training and experiences in addition to good examination results and there are class differences in the way parents choose schools, as Gewirtz et al's 1995 research shows. We have, as yet, to meet – in any of our extensive studies of parental attitudes and behaviours – many who would sacrifice good examination results for the other benefits. For example, a survey conducted for ILEA found that 78 per cent of parents thought it was very important that schools should provide their child with qualifications and only 2 per cent thought it was not important for future job prospects and further or higher education opportunities (ILEA, 1984).

We also wish to respond to the criticism that the differences between schools' academic outcomes (although statistically significant) may be so slight that they do not warrant much attention. We have identified differences which are both statistically and, more importantly, educationally significant in a number of our studies. For example, in our recent analysis of secondary school academic effectiveness the difference between the most and least effective schools (after controlling for intake) reached 12 GCSE points equivalent to the difference between 6 grade Bs and 6 grade Ds for an individual student with an average level of prior attainment at age 11. Such differences have important implications for further and higher education, as well as for employment prospects.

> Although the differences in scholastic attainment likely to he achieved by the same student in contrasting schools is unlikely to be great, in many instances, it represents the difference between success and failure and operates as a facilitating or inhibiting factor in higher education. When coupled with the promotion for other prosocial attitudes and behaviours and the inculcation of a positive self-image, the potential to improve the life chances of students is considerable
>
> (Mortimore, 1995b: 357).

The neglect of process

Some critics accuse us of ignoring the processes of schooling. Elliott, in particular, appears to believe that if the processes are 'good' then the outcomes will look after themselves (Elliott, 1996: 206). We dispute this on the grounds that educationalists still know relatively little about the relationship between teaching and learning for any individual pupil. Clearly the two are related, but the relationship is neither simple nor direct (Mortimore, 1993). Not all learning occurs in schools. Moreover, as Winch (Chapter 5, above) has argued, schools cannot be held accountable for that which they cannot influence. By focusing only on observable processes, researchers could radically misinterpret what pupils had learned. For this reason the 'touchstone' for school effectiveness studies remains the impact on pupils' educational outcomes (Reynolds, 1994). We think it is difficult, without reference to this touchstone, to evaluate different approaches to classroom organization and teaching. Without it, decisions about what constitutes 'good' practice would be made on the basis of personal taste or would depend on the whim of an 'expert'. It is interesting that the latest Framework for Inspection adopted by OFSTED also has pupil outcomes as one of its main criteria.

Our recent review of *Key Characteristics of Effective Schools* illustrates the existence of a growing body of research (we included over 160 studies in our review) which has investigated processes and identified a common core of findings. For those who have not studied the methodological details of *School Matters*, can we also point out that the majority of the project's time was spent observing classroom and social processes rather than collecting outcomes (Mortimore et al, op cit). Nonetheless, having stated our commitment to the use of outcomes, we accept the criticism that – in comparison with the number of studies focusing only on outcomes – school effectiveness research could devote more attention to process factors.

The linkage between outcomes and processes

White and Scott both raise the point that many of the factors associated with effectiveness are self-evident and that logical deduction rather than empirical research could have identified them. We believe this view is quite wrong. The correlates, identified by MLM as associated with effectiveness – at the school or department level – are far from self-evident. Fielding quotes the phrase 'empirical illustrations of tautological truths' (above, p.139), but he, too, is wide of the mark. Like both the head of OFSTED and Davies, he may believe it can all be explained by 'common sense', but he offers no evidence for this claim.

There can be many different versions of common sense, as Winch, citing Gramsci explains. How can anyone decide, other than by careful empirical research, which is the version most likely to be true? The danger with the counterview (that it is all common sense) is that this provides abundant opportunities for prejudices and particular hobby horses to be exercised. In the *Fifteen Thousand Hours* study (Rutter et al, 1979), we listed a number of commonsense items that were not supported by the evidence!

A lack of concern with equity

A number of the authors, but notably Davies, Elliott and Fielding, accuse us of ignoring questions of equity. We reject this criticism which has been made without any accompanying evidence. Those who have read the classic studies on the literature such as the article by Edmonds (1979), will know that the foundation of school effectiveness is a concern for equity. In terms of our own work, a major section of *School Matters* dealt with the lack of equity in outcomes (Mortimore et al., 1988a). A follow-up study explored, over a nine-year period, the changes occurring within gender, socio-economic and ethnic groups (Sammons, 1995).

The negative impact of social and economic disadvantage on pupils' educational opportunities is a constant theme in our work (Mortimore, 1995c; Sammons et al., 1994; Mortimore, 1996b; and Mortimore and Goldstein, 1996). Our research and that of colleagues has paid increasing attention to the concept of differential effectiveness in recent years (Nuttall et al., 1989; Goldstein, 1993; Thomas et al., 1995; and Sammons et al., 1993b and 1996b). If by their criticism Davies and the others are suggesting that, by controlling for such factors as race, class and gender, we have removed the possibility of examining for bias, they are also wrong, as we show in the concluding section of this paper.

White argues for school goals such as 'becoming self-directing citizens of a liberal, democratic society' (above, p.53). We believe that there are good arguments for emphasizing literacy, numeracy and examination achievement since much research (e.g. by the Basic Skills Unit) demonstrates that functional illiteracy and lack of numeracy prevent substantial numbers of adults from engaging in everyday activities (e.g.

reading bus or train timetables and newspapers, and understanding official documents) as well as obtaining employment. These barriers effectively prevent – or at best impede – participation in the democratic processes. We argue, therefore, that academic effectiveness is a necessary, though not, in itself, a sufficient condition for – using any acceptable definition – a good school. (See also discussions by Gray and Wilcox, 1995.) We are happy to continue our search for further factors which we can use in our school improvement work, but we reject the accusation that we have ignored the dimension of equity.

Ideological commitments

Fielding echoes the accusations made by Hamilton (1996) and by Elliott (1996) that school effectiveness researchers are supportive of most aspects of government policy and that we are uncritical of the educational reforms of recent years. 'The occupation of a political site which is by turns naive or opportunistic, and at worst complicit in a divisive model of schooling' (above, p.138).

We are surprised at this view. We trust that those who have read our corpus of work or heard our various presentations will accept that they are manifestly untrue. From the discussions of a final chapter of *School Matters* (Mortimore et al., 1988a) through the Director's Inaugural Lecture (Mortimore, 1995a) to our most recent conference presentation (Sammons et al., 1997), our stance has been evaluative: critical where our accumulated data or analyses suggest that the policy or practice is wrong and supportive where they suggest it is right. Nor have we been afraid to present our views in the public domain. Our criticisms and those of our colleagues about league tables, for instance, have been on record for a number of years (Goldstein, 1993; Sammons et al., 1993b; and Mortimore et al., 1994). Indeed, it is notable that our work for OFSTED on contextualizing school performance by taking note of the important impact of socio-economic disadvantage (Sammons et al., 1994), although initially welcomed (*TES*, 1996: 1), was later rejected in a letter by the head of OFSTED.

More seriously, Fielding quotes Elliott's accusation that research studies into school effectiveness are the 'products of an ideological commitment, rather than research, which merely provides a legitimating gloss to mask this fact' (Elliott quoted in Fielding, p.139, above).

How can anyone who understands research methodology – and who has taken the trouble to study our publications and the way we work – make such an unfair accusation? As we have noted in the previous section, we have not been afraid to speak out whenever our accumulated findings have provided reliable evidence. The descriptions of the methodology that we have used and the caveats that we have employed can be found in our various publications. We reject – utterly and completely – this accusation and challenge its makers to provide evidence for the statement or to withdraw it.

Conclusions

We believe that a number of conclusions can be drawn from theoretical papers about school effectiveness and school improvement. First, the field needs further development. More complex models are needed to reflect the complexity of the educational processes and the difficulties of studying it (Sammons, 1996). Whilst we can appreciate the value of simplicity, we feel that an over-simplistic approach is likely to mislead both practitioners and policy-makers.

Second, the crude anti-quantitative attitudes which appear amongst some of the articles need to be reconsidered. Davies's comment, for example, that 'Effectiveness studies often dehumanize students by reducing them to intake variables' is extreme and illustrates a gulf of understanding between her and ourselves. In our view, the use of MLM has enabled us to tease out the impact of a school on pupils with quite different educational backgrounds and to make the case on their behalf. We do not accept that the use of our data could dehumanize pupils more than any description or measurement does. We maintain that the availability of sophisticated data is actually more likely to help rather than harm those people from whom it is collected, hence the arguments in favour of ethnic or gender monitoring in relation to both educational and employment statistics. In general, we seek to use a range of quantitative and qualitative methods in our work, depending on the nature of the problem and the theoretical approach being employed. We believe that a combination of approaches can often be more fruitful than reliance on either in isolation.

Third, we have been surprised at the use of phrases such as Fielding's 'hegemony of school effectiveness' (p.138, above). Although the number of academics and practitioners interested in school improvement has increased remarkably over the last few years, the number of British researchers working in the field of school effectiveness remains remarkably small. Of those that do so, only a very few have undertaken any large-scale empirical work. To talk of a hegemony, therefore, appears exaggerated and partisan. Indeed, we think it highly regrettable that the country has experienced so much ideologically-driven change with so few opportunities for objective evaluation. The creation of different kinds of schools, open enrolment and the encouragement of selection, cry out for investigation within a school effectiveness framework. Only in such a way, can the claim that changes in the type of schools will lead to higher standards be properly evaluated.

We also regard it as essential that practitioners are fully involved in efforts to improve the quality of education given to young people. As we have observed in relation to recent legislative changes:

> Excellence cannot be mandated by politicians or bureaucrats. Government, central or local, would do well to realize this and ensure that any legislative framework that is created is likely to stimulate and elicit from those most involved ownership, commitment and dedication rather than learned helplessness and resentment.
>
> (Mortimore, 1995b: 357)

Finally, we wish to continue the debates with policy-makers, practitioners and with our fellow researchers. An area as important to the lives of people as education must be contestable and this includes the methods we employ to study its quality and impact (Mortimore and Stone, 1991). We believe fervently (ironically, in view of some of the criticisms reported earlier) that academics should be able to challenge the views of their peers and the government and its officials. We do not advocate a negative, responsibility-free, critical approach. Our preferred mode of operation is through constructive criticism within a context of a commitment to improvement. Ultimately, however, we must be prepared to draw on the principle of academic freedom to stand up for what our evidence tells us is true.

This does not give us or any other academics carte blanche to make political judgements on the government's or the opposition's policies. We recognize that we have no greater standing than any other citizen. In a democracy all can comment on such matters and it is only when we speak as scholars – basing our remarks on the accumulated findings of our field of study over many years or on our special training in the evaluation of evidence (Goldstein, forthcoming) – that we can make any claim to special authority. On such occasions, however, we have a duty to speak out. The 'truth versus power' debates (as a recent article in an American journal so eloquently put it) may not be comfortable for the dissenting academic but must prove worthwhile in the end. As Esdras (Chapter 4, verse 41) has stated, 'Magna est veritas, et praevalet' ('Great is truth and it prevails').

References

Acland, H. (1972), 'Streaming in English primary schools', *British Journal of Educational Psychology*, 151–9.

Adey, P. and Shayer, M. (1994), *Really Raising Standards: Cognitive Intervention and Academic Achievement*. London: Routledge.

Ainscow, M., Hargreaves, D.H., Hopkins, D., Balshaw, M., and Black-Hawkins, K. (1994), *Mapping Change in Schools: The Cambridge Manual of Research Techniques*. Cambridge: University of Cambridge Institute of Education.

Ainscow, M., Hopkins, D., Southworth, G. and West, M. (1994), *Creating the Conditions for School Improvement*. London: Fulton.

Ainsworth, M. and Batten, E. (1974), *The Effects of Environmental Factors on Secondary Educational Attainment in Manchester: A Plowden Follow-up*. London: Macmillan.

Aitkin, M., Anderson, D. and Hinde, J. (1981), 'Statistical modelling of data on teaching styles', *Journal of the Royal Statistical Society*, A 144, 4, 419–61.

Aitkin, M., Bennett, N. and Hesketh, J. (1981), 'Teaching styles and pupil progress: A re-analysis', *British Journal of Educational Psychology*, 51, 2, 170–86.

Alexander, J.C. (1995), 'Modern, anti, post and neo', *New Left Review*, 210, March/April, 63–101.

Alexander, R. (1992), *Policy and Practice in Primary Education*. London: Routledge.

— (1994), 'Wise men and clever tricks: a response', *Cambridge Journal of Education*, 24, 1, 107–12.

Alexander, R., Rose, J. and Woodhead, C. (1992), *Curriculum Organisation and Classroom Practice in Primary Schools: A Discussion Paper*. London: DES.

Angus, L. (1993), 'The sociology of school effectivenes', *British Journal of Sociology of Education*, 14, 3, 327–39.

Aristotle, *Nicomachean Ethics*.

Armor, D., Conry-Oseguera, P., Cox, M., King, N., McDonnell, L., Pascal, A., Pauly, E. and Zellman, G. (1976), *Analysis of the Reading Program in Selected Los Angeles Minority Schools*. Santa Monica: Rand.

Ball, S.J. (1990), 'Management as moral technology' in S.J. Ball (ed.), *Foucault and Education*. London: Routledge, 153–66.

— (1996), *Recreating Policy Through Qualitative Research: A Trajectory Analysis*. American Educational Research Association Annual Conference, New York, 8–12 April.

Bandura, A. (1992), *Perceived Self-efficacy in Cognitive Development and Functioning*. Invited address at the annual meeting of the American Education Research Association, San Francisco, April.

Barber, M. (1993), 'Raising standards in deprived urban areas', *National Commission on Education Briefing No. 16*, July. London: NCE.

— Barber, M. and Dann, R. (eds) (1995), *Raising Educational Standards in the Inner Cities: Practical Initiatives in Action*. London: Cassell.

Barber, M., Denning, T., Gough, G. and Johnson, M. (1995), *Urban Education Initiatives: The National Pattern*. Paper presented to the OFSTED conference, Access and Achievement in Urban Education: Nature of Improvement, 2–3 November, Bromsgrove. London: OFSTED.

Barker-Lunn, J. (1970), *Streaming in the Primary School*. Slough: NFER.

Barrow, R. and Milburn, G. (1986), *A Critical Dictionary of Educational Concepts*. Brighton: Wheatsheaf.

Beare, H., Caldwell, B.J. and Millikan, R. (1989), *Creating an Excellent School*. London: Routledge.

Bennett, N. (1976), *Teaching Styles and Pupil Progress*. London: Open Books.

— (1978), 'Recent research on teaching: a dream, a belief and a model', *British Journal of Educational Psychology*, 48, 127–47.

— (1992), *Managing Learning in the Primary Classrooms*, ASPE Paper No. 1, Stoke: Trentham Books.

Bennett, N., Summers, M. and Askew, M. (1994), 'Knowledge for teaching and teaching performance' in A. Pollard (ed.), *Look before you Leap? Research Evidence for the Curriculum at Key Stage 2*. London: Tufnell Press.

Berman, P. and McLaughlin, M. (1977), *Federal Programs Supporting Change, Vol VII: Factors Affecting Implementation and Continuation*. Santa Monica: Rand.

Bhaskar, R. (1979), *The Possibility of Naturalism*. Brighton: Harvester Press.

—   (1989), *Reclaiming Reality*. London: Verso.

Bittner, E. (1965), 'The concept of organisation', *Social Research*, 32.

Bonnett, M. (1996), 'New ERA values and the teacher–pupil relationship as a form of the poetic', *British Journal of Educational Studies*, 44, 1, March, 27–41.

Bossert, S., Dwyer, D., Rowan, B. and Lee, G. (1982), 'The instructional management role of the principal', *Educational Administration Quarterly*, 18, 34–64.

Brookover, W. and Lezotte, L. (1979), *Changes in School Characteristics Coincident with Changes in School Achievement*. East Lansing: Michigan State University.

Brookover, W., Beady, C., Flood, P., Schweitzer, J. and Wisenbaker, J. (1979), *School Social Systems and Student Achievement: Schools Can Make a Difference*. New York: Praeger.

Brophy, J. and Good, T. (1986), 'Teacher behavior and student achievement' in M.C. Wittrock (ed.), *Handbook of Research on Teaching*. New York: Macmillan.

Brown, S., Duffield, J. and Riddell, S. (1995), 'School effectiveness research: the policy makers' tool for school improvement?', *European Educational Research Association Bulletin*, 1, 1, March, 6–15.

California Assembly Office of Research (1984), *Overcoming the Odds: Making High Schools Work*. Sacramento: Author.

California State Department of Education (1980), *Report on the Special Studies of Selected ECE Schools with Increasing and Decreasing Reading Scores*. Sacramento: Office of Program Evaluation and Research.

Campbell, P., Edgar, S. and Halsted, A.L. (1994), 'Students as evaluators: a model for program evaluation', *Phi Delta Kappan*, 76, 2, October, 160–5.

Carr, D. (1994), 'Wise men and clever tricks', *Cambridge Journal of Education*, 24, 1, 89–106.

Carr, W. (1995), *For Education*. Buckingham: Open University Press.

Carr, W. and Kemmis, S. (1986), *Becoming Critical: Education, Knowledge and Action Research*. Lewes: Falmer Press.

Carroll, J. (1989), 'The Carroll model: a 25 year retrospective and prospective view', *Educational Researcher*, 18, 26–31.

Caul, L. (1994), *School Effectiveness in Northern Ireland: Illustration and Practice*. Paper for the Standing Commission on Human Rights.

Chubb, J.E. (1988), 'Why the current wave of school reform will fail', *Public Interest*, 90, 28–49.

Clegg, A. and Megson, B. (1968), *Children in Distress*. Harmondsworth: Penguin.

Cohen, M. (1983), 'Instructional, management and social conditions in effective schools', in A.O. Webb and L.D. Webb (eds) *School Finance and School Improvement: Linkages in the 1980s*. Cambridge, MA: Ballinger.

Coleman, J. S., Campbell, E., Hobson, C., McPartland, J., Mood, A., Weinfield, F. and York, R. (1966), *Equality of Educational Opportunity*. Washington: US Government Printing Office.

Coleman, J., Hoffer, T. and Kilgore, S. (1981), *Public and Private Schools*. Chicago: National Opinion Research Center.

— (1982), 'Cognitive outcomes in public and private schools', *Sociology of Education*, 55, 2/3, 65–76.

Coleman, P. (1994), *Learning about School: What Parents Need to Know and How They Can Find Out*. Institute for Research on Public Policy, Montreal, Quebec.

Coleman, P. and LaRocque, L. (1990), *Struggling to be 'Good Enough'*. London: Falmer.

Coleman, P., Collinge, J. and Seifert, T. (1993), 'Seeking the levers of change: participant attitudes and school improvement', *School Effectiveness and School Improvement*, 4, 1, 59–83.

Coleman, P., Collinge, J. and Tabin, Y. (1994), *Improving Schools From the Inside Out: A Progress Report on the Coproduction of Learning Project in British Columbia, Canada*. Faculty of Education, Simon Fraser University, Burnaby, BC, Canada.

Creemers, B.P.M. (1994), 'The history, value and purpose of school effectiveness studies' in D. Reynolds, B.P.M. Creemers, P.S. Nesselradt, E.C. Shaffer, S. Stringfield and C. Teddlie (eds) *Advances in School Effectiveness Research and Practice*. Oxford: Pergamon.

Creemers, B. and Scheerens, J. (eds) (1989), 'Development in school effectiveness research', special edition of *International Journal of Education Research*, 13, 685–825.

Creemers, B.., Reynolds, D. and Swint, F.E. (1994), *The International School Effectiveness Research Programme ISERP First Results of the Quantitative Study*. Paper presented at the British Education Research Association conference, Oxford, September.

Cuban, L. (1984), 'Transforming the frog into a prince: effective schools research, policy and practice at district level', *Harvard Educational Review*, 54, 2, 129–51.

Cuttance, P. (1987), *Modelling Variation in the Effectiveness of Schooling*. Edinburgh: Centre for Educational Sociology.

Dale, R. and Fielding, M. (1989), 'Overview of section two: case studies and initiatives' in C. Harber and R. Meighan (eds) *The Democratic School: Educational Management and the Practice of Democracy*. Ticknall: Education Now Books.

Daly, P. (1991), 'How large are secondary school effects in Northern Ireland?', *School Effectiveness and School Improvement*, 2, 4, 305–23.

Davies, L. (1994), *Beyond Authoritarian School Management*. Ticknall: Education Now Books.

— (1995), 'International indicators of democratic schools' in C. Harber (ed.), *Developing Democratic Education*. Ticknall: Education Now Books.

— (1996), 'The management and mismanagement of school effectiveness' in J. Turner (ed.), *The State and the School: An International Perspective*. London: Falmer Press.

de Jong, M. (1988), *Educational Climate and Achievement in Dutch Schools*. Paper presented at the International Conference for Effective Schools, London.

Dearden, R.F., Hirst, P.H. and Peters R.S. (1972), *Education and the Development of Reason*. London: Routledge & Kegan Paul.

Department for Education (1992), *Choice and Diversity: A New Framework for Schools*. London: DFE.

— (1995), *Value Added in Education: A Briefing Paper from the Department for Education*. London: HMSO.

Department of Education and Science Inspectorate of Schools (1977), *Ten Good Schools: A Secondary School Enquiry*. London: HMSO.

Development of African Education (DAE), (1995), *DAE Newsletter*, 7, 3, July–September.

Doyle, W. (1985), 'Effective secondary classroom practices' in M. Kyle (ed.), *Reaching for Excellence: An Effective Schools Sourcebook*. Washington DC: US Government Printing Office

— (1986), 'Classroom organization and management' in M.C. Wittrock (ed.), *Handbook of Research on Teaching* (3rd edition). New York: MacMillan.

Dreyfus, H.L. and Rabinow, P. (1982), *Michel Foucault: Beyond Structuralism and Hermeneutics*. Brighton: Harvester Press.

Edmonds, R. (1979), 'Effective schools for the urban poor', *Educational Leadership*, 37, 1, 15–27.

— (1981), 'Making public schools effective', *Social Policy*, 12, 56–60.

Elliott, J. (1983), 'Self-evaluation, professional development and accountability', in M. Galton and B. Moon (eds) *Changing Schools … Changing Curriculum*. London: Harper & Row.

— (1996), 'School effectiveness research and its critics: alternative visions of schooling', *Cambridge Journal of Education*, 26, 2, 199–224.

Elwood, J. (1996), 'Undermining gender stereotypes: examination and coursework performance in the UK at 16', *Assessment in Education*, 2, 3, 283–303.

Entwistle, N. (1990), *Handbook of Educational Ideas and Practices*. London: Routledge.

Epstein, J.L. (1987), 'Effects of teacher practices and parent involvement on student achievement in reading and maths' in S. Silver (ed.), *Literacy through Family Community and School Interaction*. Greenich, CT: JAI Press.

Evertson, C., Emmer, E. and Brophy, J. (1980), 'Predictors of effective teaching in junior high mathematics classrooms', *Journal for Research in Mathematics Education*, 11, 3, 167–78.

Fielding, M. (1989), 'Democracy and fraternity: towards a new paradigm for the comprehensive school' in H. Lauder and P. Brown (eds) *Education: In Search of a Future*. Lewes: Falmer Press, 50–74.

— (1994), 'Delivery, packages and the denial of learning: reversing the language and practice of contemporary INSET' in H. Bradley, C. Conner and G. Southworth (eds) *Developing Teachers Developing Schools*. London: Fulton, 18–33.

— (1995), *Mapping the Progress of Change*. Annual meeting of the British Educational Research Association and European conference on Educational Research, Bath, 17 September.

— (1996a), *School Cultures: Struggling to Develop New Understandings*. Workshop paper at the annual conference of the Philosophy of Education Society of Great Britain, New College, Oxford, 29–31 March.

— (1996b), *Mapping Change in Schools: Developing a New Methodology – From School Improvement to Transformative Education*. Annual conference of the American Educational Research Association, New York, 8–12 April.

— (1996c), 'Empowerment: emancipation or enervation?', *Journal of Education Policy*, 11, 3, 399–417.

Finn, C. (1984), 'Towards strategic independence: nine commandments for enhancing school effectiveness', *Phi Delta Kappan*, 65, 8, 518–24.

Firestone, W.A. (1991), 'Introduction: Chapter 1' in J.R. Bliss, W.A. Firestone and C.E. Richards (eds) *Rethinking Effective Schools: Research and Practice*. Englewood Cliffs, New Jersey: Prentice Hall.

Fitz-Gibbon, C.T. (1990), 'Analysing examination results' in C.T. Fitz-Gibbon (ed.), *Performance Indicators*. Clevedon: Multilingual Matters.

— (1991), 'Multilevel modelling in an indicator system' in S.W. Rauderbush and J.D. Willms (eds) *Schools, Classrooms and Pupils: International Studies of Schooling from a Multilevel Perspective*. San Diego: Academic Press.

—   (1992), 'School effects at A level: genesis of an information system' in D. Reynolds and P. Cuttance (eds) *School Effectiveness Research, Policy and Practice*. London: Cassell.

Fraser, B.J., Walberg, H.J., Welch, W.W. and Hattie, J.A. (1987), 'Syntheses of educational productivity research', *International Journal of Educational Research*, 11, 2, 145–252.

Fullan, M.G. (1991), *The New Meaning of Educational Change*. London: Cassell.

Fullan, M. and Hargreaves, D. (1992), *What's Worth Fighting for in Your School?* Buckingham: Open University Press.

Fuller, B. (1991), *Growing Up Modern: the Western State builds Third World Schools*. New York: Routledge.

Fuller, B. and Clarke, P. (1994), 'Raising school effects while ignoring culture? Local conditions and the influence of classroom tools, rules and pedagogy', *Review of Educational Research*, 64, 119–57.

Gadamer, H.-G. (1975), *Truth and Method*. London: Sheed and Word.

Galton, M. and Simon, B. (1980), *Inside the Primary Classroom*. London: Routledge & Kegan Paul.

Gewirtz, S., Ball, S. and Bowe, R. (1995), *Markets, Choice and Equality in Education*. Buckingham: Open University.

Giddens, A. (1984), *The Constitution of Society*. Cambridge: Polity Press.

Gipps, C. (1992), *What We Know about Effective Primary Teaching*. London: Tufnell Press.

—   (1994), *Beyond Testing: Towards a Theory of Educational Assessment*. London: Falmer Press.

Gipps, C. and Murphy, P. (1995), *A Fair Test? Assessment and Equity*. Buckingham: Open University Press.

Glenn, B. (1981), *What Works? An Examination of Effective Schools for Poor Black Children*. Cambridge, MA: Harvard University Center for Law and Education.

Glickman, C. (1987), 'Good and/or effective schools: what do we want?', *Phi Delta Kappan*, 68, 8, April, 622–4.

—   (1991), 'Pretending not to know what we know', *Educational Leadership*, 48, 8, May, 4–10.

—   (1993), *Renewing America's Schools: A Guide for School-Based Action*. San Francisco: Jossey Bass.

Goldstein, H. (1987), *Multilevel Models in Educational and Social Research*. London: Griffin, Oxford University Press.

— (1997), Response to Hargreaves on 'Evidence-based educational research', *Research Intelligence*, February, 59:18-20.

Goldstein, H. and Sammons, P. (1995), *The Influence of Secondary and Junior Schools on Sixteen Year Examination Performance: A Cross-classified Multilevel Analysis*. London: Institute of Education.

Goldstein, H. and Spiegelhalter, D. (1996), 'League tables and their limitations: statistical issues in comparisons of institutional performance', *Journal of the Royal Statistical Society A*, 159, 3, 385–443.

Goldstein, H. and Thomas, S. (1995), 'School effectiveness and "value added" analysis', *Forum*, 37, 2, 36–8.

— (1996), 'Using examination results as indicators of school and college performance', *Journal of the Royal Statistical Society*, 159, 1, 149–63.

Goldstein, H., Rasbash, J., Yang, M., Woodhouse, G., Pan, H., Nuttall, D. and Thomas, S. (1993), 'A multilevel analysis of school examination results', *Oxford Review of Education*, 19, 4, 425–33.

Good, T. (1984), 'Teacher effects' in *Making Our Schools More Effective: Proceedings of Three State Conferences*. University of Missouri.

Goodlad, J (1984), *A Place Called School: Prospects for the Future*. New York: McGraw Hill.

Grace, G. (1995), *School Leadership: Beyond Education Management*. London: Falmer Press.

Gramsci, A. (1971), *Selections from the Prison Notebooks* in Q. Hoare and G. Nowell-Smith (eds). London: Lawrence and Wishart.

Gray, J. (1981), 'A competitive edge: examination results and the probable limits of secondary school effectiveness', *Educational Review*, 33, 1, 25–35.

— (1990), 'The quality of schooling: frameworks for judgements', *British Journal of Educational Studies*, 38, 3, 204–33.

— (1993), 'Review of Scheerens, J. (1992), "Effective Schooling: Research, Theory and Practice"', *School Effectiveness and School Improvement*, 4, 3, 230–5.

Gray, J. and Wilcox, B. (1994), *The Challenge of Turning round Ineffective Schools*. Paper presented to the ESRC seminar series on school effectiveness and school improvement, Newcastle University, October 1994.

— (1995), *Good School, Bad School*. Buckingham: Open University Press.

Gray, J., Jesson, D. and Jones, B. (1986), 'The search for a fairer way of comparing schools' examination results', *Research Papers in Education*, 1, 2, 91–122.

Gray, J., Jesson, D. and Sime, N. (1990), 'Estimating differences in the examination performance of secondary schools in six LEAs: A multilevel approach to school effectiveness', *Oxford Review of Education*, 16, 2, 137–58.

Gray, J., Jesson, D., Goldstein, H., Hedger, K. and Rasbash, J. (1993), *A Multi-level Analysis of School Improvement: Changes in Schools' Performance Over Time*. Paper presented at the fifth European conference of the European Association for Research on Learning and Instruction, 3 September, Aix-en-Provence, France.

Gray, J., McPherson, A. and Raffe, D. (1983), *Reconstructions of Secondary Education*. London: Routledge & Kegan Paul.

Hall, S. (1993), 'Thatcherism today', *New Statesman and Society*, 26 November.

Hallinger, P. and Leithwood, K. (1994), 'Introduction: exploring the impact of principal leadership', *School Effectiveness and School Improvement*, 5, 3, 206–18.

Hallinger, P. and Murphy, J. (1985), 'Instructional leadership and school socio-economic status: a preliminary investigation', *Administrator's Notebook*, 31, 5, 1–4.

—   (1986), 'The social context of effective schools', *American Journal of Education*, 94, 3, 328–55.

Hamilton, D. (1994), *Clockwork Universes and Oranges*. Paper on the future of educational research presented to the annual conference of the British Educational Research Association, 9 September, St Anne's College, Oxford.

—   (1996), 'Peddling feel-good fictions', summer *Forum* 38, 2, 54–6.

Hamlyn, D. (1967), 'Logical and psychological aspects of learning' in R.S. Peters (ed.), *The Concept of Education*. London: Routledge & Kegan Paul.

Hammersley, M. (1992), *What's Wrong with Ethnography?* London: Routledge.

Hanford, G.H. (1986), 'The SAT and state-wide assessment: sorting the uses and caveats' in *Commentaries on Testing*, Princeton, NJ, College Entrance Examination Board.

Hanushek, E. (1979), 'Conceptual and empirical issues in the estimation of educational production functions', *Journal of Human Resources*, 14, 351–88.

—   (1986), 'The economics of schooling: production and efficiency in public schools', *Journal of Economic Literature*, 24, 1141–77.

—   (1989), 'The impact of differential expenditures on school performance', *Educational Researcher* 18, 4, 45–65.

Harber, C. (1995), 'Democratic education and the international agenda' in C. Harber (ed.), *Developing Democratic Education*. Ticknall: Education Now Books.

Hargreaves, A. (1994), *Changing Teachers, Changing Times*. London: Cassell.

Harris, A., Jamieson, I. and Russ, J. (1996), *School Effectiveness and School Improvement: A Practical Guide*. London: Pitman.

Heal, K. (1978), 'Misbehaviour among school children: the role of the school in strategies for prevention', *Policy and Politics*, 6, 321–33.

Hedges, L.V., Laine, R.D. and Greenwald, R. (1994), 'Does money matter? A meta-analysis of studies of the effects of differential school inputs on student outcomes (an exchange: part 1)', *Educational Researcher*, 23, 3, 5–14.

Helmreich, R. (1972), 'Stress, self-esteem and attitudes' in B. King and E. McGinnies (eds) *Attitudes, Conflict and Social Change*. London: Academic Press.

Hersh, R., Carnine, D., Gall, M., Stockard, J., Carmack, M. and Gannon, P. (1981), *The Management of Education Professionals in Instructionally Effective Schools: Towards A Research Agenda*. Eugene: Center for Educational Policy and Management, University of Oregon.

HMSO (1995), *Schools under Scrutiny: Strategies for the Evaluation of School Performance*. London, Paris: OECD Publications.

Hobsbaum, A. and Hillman, J. (1994), *Reading Recovery in England*. London: Institute of Education.

Holmes, M. (1989), 'From research to implementation to improvement' in M. Holmes, K.A. Leithwood and D.F. Musella (eds) *Educational Policy for Effective Schools*. New York: Teachers College Press.

Hopkins, D. (1994), *Towards a Theory for School Improvement*. Paper presented to the ESRC seminar series on school effectiveness and school improvement, Newcastle University, October.

Hopkins, D., Ainscow, M. and West, M. (1994), *School Improvement in an Era of Change*. London: Cassell.

— (1996), *Improving the Quality of Education for All*. London: Fulton.

ILEA (1984), *Improving Secondary Schools*. Research study, conducted for the Hargreaves Report, ILEA: London.

Jansen, J. (1995), 'Effective schools?', *Comparative Education*, 31, 2, 181–200.

Jencks, C.S., Smith, M., Ackland, H., Bane, M.J., Cohen, D., Gintis, H., Heyns, B. and Micholson, S. (1972), *Inequality: Assessment of the Effect of Family and Schooling in America*. New York: Basic Books.

Jesson, D. and Gray, J. (1991), 'Slants on slopes: using multi-level models to investigate differential school effectiveness and its impact on pupils' examination results', *School Effectiveness and School Improvement*, 2, 3, 230–71.

Jones, K. (1996), 'Will they ever learn?' *Red Pepper*, 30, November, 13–15.

Jowett, S., Baginsky, M. and MacDonald, M. (1991), *Building Bridges: Parental Involvement in Schools*. Windsor: NFER-Nelson.

Joyce, B. (1991), 'The doors to school improvement', *Educational Leadership*, 48, 8, 59–62.

Joyce, B. and Showers, B. (1988), *Student Achievement Through Staff Development*. New York: Longman.

Joyce, J. (1960), *A Portrait of the Artist as a Young Man*. Harmondsworth: Penguin Books.

Lee, V., Bryk, A. and Smith, J. (1993), 'The organisation of effective secondary schools' in L. Darling-Hammond (ed.), *Research in Education*, 19, 171–226. Washington DC: American Educational Research Association.

Levin, H. and Lockheed, M. (eds) (1993), *Effective Schools in Developing Countries*. London: Falmer Press.

Levine, D. (1992), 'An interpretive review of US research and practice dealing with unusual effective schools' in D. Reynolds and P. Cuttance (eds) *School Effectiveness Research, Policy and Practice*. London: Cassell.

Levine, D. and Stark, J. (1981), *Instructional and Organisational Arrangements and Processes for Improving Academic Achievement at Inner City Elementary Schools*. Kansas City: University of Missouri.

Levine, D.U. and Lezotte, L.W. (1990), *Unusually Effective Schools: A Review and Analysis of Research and Practice*. Madison, WI: National Centre for Effective Schools Research and Development.

Lezotte, L. (1989), 'School improvement based on the effective schools research', *International Journal of Educational Research*, 13, 7, 815–25.

Lightfoot, S. (1983), *The Good High School: Portraits of Character and Culture*. New York: Basic Books.

Lipsitz, J. (1984), *Successful Schools for Young Adolescents*. New Brunswick: Transaction Books.

Little, A. and Sivisathambaran, R. (1993), 'Improving educational effectiveness in a plantation school: the case of the Gonakelle School in Sri Lanka' in H. Levin and M. Lockheed (eds) *Effective Schools in Developing Countries*. London: Falmer Press.

Louis, K.S. and Marks, S. (1995), *Professionalism and Community*. Thousand Oaks, CA: Corwin Press.

Louis, K.S. and Miles, M.B. (1991), 'Toward effective urban high schools: the importance of planning and coping' in J.R. Bliss, W.A. Firestone and C.E. Richards (eds) *Rethinking Effective Schools: Research and Practice*. Englewood Cliffs, New Jersey: Prentice Hall.

—   (1992), *Improving the Urban High School: What Works and Why*. London: Cassell.

Luyten, H. (1994), *Stability of School Effects in Secondary Education: The Impact of Variance across Subjects and Years*. Paper presented at the annual meeting of the American Educational Research Association, 4–8 April, New Orleans.

Lwehabura, J. (1993), 'School Effectiveness and Self-Reliance in Tanzania'. Unpublished PhD thesis, University of Birmingham.

MacBeath, J. (1994), *Making Schools More Effective: A Role for Parents in School Self-evaluation and Development*. Planning paper presented to annual conference of the American Educational Research Association, 4–8 April, New Orleans.

MacBeath, J. and Mortimore, P. (1994), *Improving School Effectiveness: A Scottish Approach*. Paper presented at the annual conference of the British Educational Research Association, 9 September, St Anne's College, Oxford.

MacGilchrist, B. (1995), *The Use of Qualitative Data in an Empirical Study of School Development Planning*. Paper presented at ICSEI, 3–6 January, Leeuwarden, The Netherlands, London: ISEIC, Institute of Education.

MacGilchrist, B., Mortimore. P., Savage, J. and Beresford, C. (1995), *Planning Matters*. London: Paul Chapman.

MacIntyre, A. (1981), *After Virtue*. London: Duckworth.

MacKenzie, D. (1983), 'Research for school improvement: an appraisal of some recent trends', *Educational Researcher*, 12, 4, 5–16.

Madaus, G.G., Kellagham, T., Rakow, E.A. and King, D. (1979), 'The sensitivity of measures of school effectiveness', *Harvard Educational Review*, 49, 207–30.

Mayston, D. and Jesson, D. (1988), 'Developing models of educational accountability', *Oxford Review of Education*, 14, 3.

McClaren, P. (1995), *Critical Pedagogy and Predatory Culture*. London and New York: Routledge.

McDill, E. and Rigsby, L. (1973), *Structure and Process in Secondary Schools*. Baltimore: John Hopkins University Press.

McGaw, B., Banks, D. and Piper, K. (1991), *Effective Schools: Schools that Make a Difference*. Melbourne: Australian Council for Educational Research.

McGaw, B., Piper, K., Banks, D. and Evans, B. (1992), *Making Schools More Effective*. Melbourne: Australian

McMahon, A., Bolam, R., Abbott, R. and Holly, P. (1984), *Guidelines for Review and Internal Development in Schools* (Primary and Secondary School Handbooks). York: Longman/Schools Council.

McPherson, A. (1992), 'Measuring added value in schools', *National Commission on Education Briefing No. 1*, February, London.

Miles, M., Farrar, E. and Neufeld, E. (1983), 'Review of Effective School Programs, Vol 2: The Extent of Effective School Programs'. Cambridge MA: Huron Institute (unpublished).

Mill, J.S. (1910), *On Liberty*. London: Dent.

Mortimore, P. (1991a), 'School effectiveness research: which way at the crossroads?', *School Effectiveness and School Improvement*, 2, 3, 213–29.

—   (1991b), 'The nature and findings of research on school effectiveness in the primary sector' in S. Riddell and S. Brown (eds) *School Effectiveness Research: Its Message for School Improvement*. Edinburgh: Scottish Office Education Department, 9–19.

—   (1991c), 'Effective schools from a British perspective' in J.R. Bliss, W.A. Firestone and C.E. Richards (1991), *Rethinking Effective Schools: Research and Practice*. Englewood Cliffs, New Jersey: Prentice Hall.

—   (1992), 'Issues in school effectiveness', in D. Reynolds and P. Cuttance (eds) *School Effectiveness Research, Policy and Practice*. London: Cassell.

—   (1993), 'School effectiveness and the management of effective learning and teaching', *School Effectiveness and School Improvement*, 4, 4, 290–310.

—   (1994), 'The positive effects of schooling' in M. Rutter (ed.), *Youth in the Year 2000: Psycho-social Issues and Interventions*. Boston: Cambridge University Press.

—   (1995a), *Effective Schools: Current Impact and Future Possibilities*. The Director's Inaugural Lecture, London: Institute of Education. University of London, February.

—   (1995b), 'The positive effects of schooling', in M. Rutter (ed.), *Psycho-Social Disturbances in Young People: Challenges for Prevention*. Cambridge: Cambridge University Press.

—   (1995c), 'Better than excuses', *TES*, July, 17.

—   (1996a), *Partnership and Cooperation in School Improvement*. Paper presented at the conference of the Association for Teacher Education in Europe, Glasgow, Scotland, September.

—   (1996b), *Redressing Disadvantage*. Lewisham headteachers' conference, Hythe, November.

Mortimore, P. and Goldstein, H. (1996), *The Teaching of Reading in 45 Inner London Secondary Schools: A Critical Examination of OFSTED Research*. London: Institute of Education.

Mortimore, P. and Stone, C. (1991), 'Measuring educational quality', *British Journal of Educational Studies*, 34, 1, 69–73.

Mortimore, P., Sammons, P. and Ecob, R. (1988c), 'Expressing the magnitude of school effects', a reply to Peter Preece, *Research Papers in Education*, 3, 2, 99–101.

Mortimore, P. Sammons, P. and Thomas, S. (1994), 'School effectiveness and value added measures', *Assessment in Education*, 1, 3, 315–32.

Mortimore, P., Sammons, P. and Thomas, S. (1995), 'School effectiveness and value added measures: a paper presented at the Desmond Nuttall Memorial Conference, 10 June 1994', *Assessment in Education: Principles, Policy and Practice*, 1, 3, 315–32.

Mortimore, P., Sammons, P., Stoll, L., Lewis, D. and Ecob, R. (1987a), 'Towards more effective junior schooling', summer *Forum*, 29, 3, 70–3.

— (1987b), 'For effective classroom practices', autumn *Forum*, 30, 1, 8–11.

— (1987c), 'The ILEA junior school project: a study of school effectiveness', spring *Forum*, 29, 2, 47–9.

— (1988), *School Matters: The Junior Years*. Wells: Open Books.

Mortimore, P., Sammons, P., Stoll, L., Lewis, D. and Ecob, R. (1988a), *School Matters: The Junior Years*. Wells: Open Books.

— (1988b), 'The effects of school membership on pupils' educational outcomes', *Research Papers in Education*, 3, 1, 3–26.

Murphy, J. (1989), 'Principal instructional leadership' in P. Thuston and L. Lotto (eds) *Advances in Educational Leadership*. Greenich: JAI Press.

Myers, K. (forthcoming), *School Improvement in Practice: Schools Make a Difference*. London: Falmer Press.

Myers, K. and Goldstein, H. (1996), 'Get it in context?' *Education*, 16 February, 187/7.

National Commission on Education (1996), *Success Against the Odds: Effective Schooling in Disadvantaged Areas* (eds) J. Hillman and M. Madden, London: Routledge.

National Institute of Education (1978), *Violent Schools – Safe Schools: The Safe School Study Report to the Congress*. Washington DC: Department of Health, Education and Welfare.

North West Regional Educational Laboratory (1990), *Onward to Excellence: Effective Schooling Practices: A Research Synthesis*. Portland, Oregon: North West Regional Educational Laboratory.

Nuttall, D. (1995), in R. Murphy and P. Broadfoot (eds) *Effective Assessment and the Improvement of Education: A Tribute to Desmond Nuttall*. London: Falmer Press.

Nuttall, D., Goldstein, H., Prosser, R. and Rasbash, J. (1989), 'Differential school effectiveness', *International Journal of Educational Research*, special issue Developments in School Effectiveness Research, 13, 769–76.

O'Hear, A. (1982), *Education, Society and Human Nature*. London: Routledge & Kegan Paul.

O'Hear, P. and White, J. (1991), *A National Curriculum for All*. London: Institute of Public Policy Research.

OFSTED (1993), *Access and Achievement in Urban Education*. London: HMSO.

— (1994), *Handbook for the Inspection of Schools*, Part 4, 9–10, 48. London: HMSO.

Omari, I. and Mosha, H. (1987), *The Quality of Primary Education in Tanzania*. Nairobi: Mangraphics Ltd.

Paterson, L. and Goldstein, H. (1991), 'New statistical methods of analysing social structures: an introduction to multilevel models', *British Educational Research Journal*, 17, 4, 387–93.

Pearson, A. (1989), *The Teacher: Theory and Practice in Teacher Education*. London: Routledge.

Perrone, V. (1989), *Working Papers: Reflections on Teachers, Schools And Community*. New York: Teachers College Press. (See especially 'Effective schools, teaching and learning', 37–49.)

Peters, R.S. and White, J. (1969), 'The philosopher's contribution to educational research', *Educational Philosophy and Theory*, 1.

Phillips, M. (1996), 'Inspectors only come under fire when they say schools are doing badly: no-one complains about their methods when the results are good', *Observer*, 27 October, 2.

Pollack, S., Watson, D. and Chrispeels, J. (1987), *A Description of Factors and Implementation Strategies Used by Schools in Becoming Effective for all Students*. Paper for American Educational Research Association.

Powell, M. (1980), 'The beginning teacher evaluation study: a brief history of a major research project' in C. Denham and A. Lieberman (eds) *Time to Learn*. Washington DC: National Institute of Education.

Preece, P. (1989), 'Pitfalls in research on school and teacher effectiveness', *Research Papers in Education*, 4, 3, 47–69.

Pring, R. (1994), 'Liberal education and vocational education: a conflict of value' in H. Haldane (ed.), *Education, Values and the State*. St Andrews: Centre for Philosophy and Public Affairs University of St Andrews, 7–41.

— (1995), *Educating Persons: Putting 'Education' Back into Educational Research*. Lecture to the annual conference of the Scottish Educational Research Association, September.

Purkey, S.C. and Smith, M.S. (1983), 'Effective schools: a review', *Elementary School Journal*, 83, 4, 427–52.

Ralph, J.H. and Fennessey, J. (1983), 'Science or reform: some questions about the effective schools model', *Phi Delta Kappan*, 64, 10, 589–694.

Reid, K., Hopkins, D. and Holly, P. (1987), *Towards the Effective School*. Oxford: Blackwell.

Reynolds, D. (1976), 'The delinquent school' in P. Woods (ed.), *The Process of Schooling*. London: Routledge & Kegan Paul.

— (1982), 'The search for effective schools', *School Organisation*, 2, 3, 215–37.

— (1989), 'School effectiveness and school improvement: a review of the British literature' in D. Reynolds, B. Creemers and T. Peters (eds) *School Effectiveness and Improvement*. Proceedings of the First International Congress, London, 1988. Cardiff: School of Education, University of Wales, College of Cardiff.

— (1992), 'School effectiveness and school improvement: an updated review of the British literature' in D. Reynolds and P. Cuttance (eds) *School Effectiveness Research, Policy and Practice*. London: Cassell.

— (1994), Inaugural Lecture, University of Newcastle-upon-Tyne, October.

— (1995), 'Failure free schooling', Melbourne: *IARTV Series*, 49.

Reynolds, D. and Creemers, B. (1990), 'School effectiveness and school improvement: a mission statement', *School Effectiveness and School Improvement*, 1, 1, 1–3.

Reynolds, D. and Cuttance, P. (eds) (1992), *School Effectiveness Research, Policy and Practice*. London: Cassell.

Reynolds, D. and Murgatroyd, S. (1977), 'The sociology of schooling and the absent pupil: the school as a factor in the generation of truancy' in H. Carroll (ed.), *Absenteeism in South Wales: Studies of Pupils, their Homes and their Secondary Schools*. University College of Swansea, Faculty of Education.

Reynolds, D. and Packer, A. (1992), 'School effectiveness and school improvement in the 1990s' in D. Reynolds and P. Cuttance (eds) *School Effectiveness Research, Policy and Practice*. London: Cassell.

Reynolds, D., Hopkins, D. and Stoll, L. (1993), 'Linking school effectiveness knowledge and school improvement practice: towards a synergy', *School*.

— Reynolds, D. et al. (1994), 'School effectiveness research: a review of the international literature' in D. Reynolds, B.P.M. Creemers, P.S. Nesselradt, E.C. Schaffer, S. Stringfield and C.Teddlie (eds) *Advances in School Effectiveness Research and Practice*. Oxford: Pergamon.

Reynolds, D., Creemers, B., Nesselrodt, P.S., Schaffer, E.C., Stringfield, S. and Teddlie, C. (1994), *Advances in School Effectiveness Research and Practice*. Oxford: Pergamon.

Riddell, S., Brown, S. and Duffield, J. (1994), *The Social and Institutional Context of Effectiveness*. Paper presented at the annual conference of the British Educational Research Association, St Anne's College, Oxford, September 1994.

—   (1996), *The Utility of Qualitative Research for Influencing Policy and Practice on School Effectiveness*. Annual conference of the American Educational Research Association, New York, 8–12 April.

Robertson, P., Sammons P. and Mortimore, P. (1996), *Improving School Effectiveness: A Project in Progress*. Paper presented at the BERA annual conference, Lancaster, September.

Rosenshine, B. (1987), 'Direct instruction' in M.J. Dunkin (ed.), *The International Encyclopedia of Teaching and Teacher Education*. Oxford: Pergamon Press.

Rosenshine, B. and Berliner, D. (1978), 'Academic engaged time', *British Journal of Teacher Education*, 4, 3–16.

Rosenshine, B. and Stevens, R. (1981), 'Advances in Research on Teaching'. Unpublished manuscript, University of Illinois.

Rudduck, J. (1991), *Innovation and Change*. Milton Keynes: Open University Press.

Rutter, M. (1983), 'School effects on pupil progress – findings and policy implications', *Child Development*, 54, 1, 1–29.

Rutter, M., Maughan, B., Mortimore, P. and Ouston, J. (1979), *Fifteen Thousand Hours: Secondary Schools and their Effects on Children*. London: Open Books.

Sammons, P. (1987), *Findings from School Effectiveness Research: A Framework for School Improvement*. Keynote paper presented to the annual convention of the Prince Edward Island Teachers' Federation on 'School Atmosphere: The Barometer of Success', Charlottetown, Prince Edward Island, Canada, 29–30 October.

—   (1994), 'Findings from school effectiveness research: some implications for improving the quality of schools' in P. Ribbins and E. Burridge (eds) *Improving Education: The Issue in Quality*. London: Cassell.

—   (1995), 'Gender, ethnic and socio-economic differences in attainment and progress: a longitudinal analysis of student achievement over 9 years', *British Educational Research Journal*, 21, 4, 465–85.

—   (1996), 'Complexities in the judgement of school effectiveness', *Educational Research and Evaluation*, 2, 2, 113–49.

Sammons, P. and Hillman, J. (1994e), *Markets for Secondary Schools: The Interaction of LMS, Open Enrolment and Examination Results*. Proposal submitted to the Nuffield Foundation, London: ISEIC, Institute of Education.

Sammons, P. and Reynolds, D. (1997), 'A partisan evaluation – John Elliott on school effectiveness', *Cambridge Journal of Education*, spring.

Sammons, P., Hillman, J. and Mortimore, P. (1995), *Key Characteristics of Effective Schools: A Review of School Effectiveness Research*. Report commissioned for the Office for Standards in Education. London: Institute of Education and OFSTED.

Sammons, P., Mortimore, P. and Hillman, J. (1996a), 'Key characteristics of effective schools: a response to 'Peddling feel-good fictions', *Forum*, 38, 3, 88–90.

Sammons, P., Mortimore, P. and Hillman, J. (1996b), 'A response to David Hamilton's reflections', *Forum*, 31, 3, 88–90.

Sammons, P., Mortimore, P. and Thomas, S. (1993a), *Do Schools Perform Consistently across Outcomes and Areas?* Paper presented to the ESRC seminar series 'School Effectiveness and School Improvement', July 1993, University of Sheffield.

— (1993b), 'First weigh your ingredients', *The Independent*, 20 November.Sammons, P. Nuttall, D. and Cuttance, P. (1993a), 'Differential school effectiveness: results from a reanalysis of the Inner London Education Authority's junior school project data', *British Educational Research*, 19, 4, 381–405.

Sammons, P., Cuttance, P., Nuttall, D. and Thomas, S. (1994a), *Continuity of School Effects: A Longitudinal Analysis of Primary and Secondary School Effects on GCSE Performance*. Originally presented at the Sixth International Congress for School Effectiveness and Improvement, Norrkoping, Sweden and revised version submitted to *School Effectiveness and School Improvement*.

Sammons, P., Thomas, S. and Mortimore, P. (1995b), *Accounting for Variations in Academic Effectiveness Between Schools and Departments: Results from the 'Differential Secondary School Effectiveness Project': A Three Year Study of GCSE Performance*. Paper presented at the European conference on Educational Research/BERA Annual Conference, Bath, 14–17 September.

— (1996a), *Towards a Model of Academic Effectiveness for Secondary Schools*. Paper presented to the annual conference of the British Educational Research Association, University of Lancaster.

— (1996b), *Differential School Effectiveness: Departmental Variations in GCSE Attainment*. Paper presented at AERA annual conference, New York, April (submitted to *The School Field*).

— (1997), *School and Departmental Effectiveness: Implications from a Recent British Study for Policy, Practice and Future Research*. Paper presented at ICSEI, Memphis, January 1997. (To appear as Chapter 9 in *Effective Schools: Effective Departments*. Paul Chapman – forthcoming).

Sammons, P., Lewis, A., MacLure, M., Riley, J., Bennett, N. and Pollard, A. (1994d), 'Teaching and learning processes' in A. Pollard (ed.), *Look before you leap? Research evidence for the curriculum at Key Stage 2*. London: Tufnell Press.

Sammons, P., Thomas, S., Mortimore, P., Cairns, R. and Bausor, J. (1994), *Understanding the Processes of School and Departmental Effectiveness*. Paper presented to the annual conference of the British Educational Research Association, 9 September, St Anne's College, Oxford.

Sammons, P., Thomas, S., Mortimore, P., Owen, C. and Pennell, H. (1994b), *Assessing School Effectiveness: Developing Measures to put School Performance in Context*. London: OFSTED.

Sanday, A. (1990), *Making schools more effective (CEDAR Papers 2)*. Warwick: Centre for Educational Development, Appraisal and Research, University of Warwick.

Scheerens, J. (1992), *Effective Schooling: Research, Theory and Practice*, London: Cassell.

Scheffler, I. (1960), *The Language of Education*. Springfield: Charles C. Thomas.

Schweitzer, J. (1984), *Characteristics of effective schools*. Paper for American Educational Research Association.

Scott, D. and Usher, R. (eds) (1996), *Understanding Educational Research*. London: Routledge.

Selleck, R.J.W. (1972), *English Primary Education and the Progressives 1914–1939*. London: Routledge.

Silver, H. (1994)*Good Schools, Effective Schools*. London: Cassell. (See especially 'Effective schools: a research movement', Chapter 6.)

Sizemore, B. (1985), 'Pitfalls and promises of effective schools research', *Journal of Negro Education*, 54, 3, 269–88.

— (1987), 'The effective African American elementary school' in G. Noblit and W. Pink (eds) *Schooling in a Social Context: Qualitative Studies*. Norwood, NJ: Ablex.

Sizemore, B., Brossard, C. and Harrigan, B. (1983), *An Abashing Anomaly: The High Achieving Predominantly Black Elementary School*. University of Pittsburgh.

Slavin, R.E. (1987), 'A theory of school and classroom organisation', *Educational Psychologist*, 22, 2, 89–108.

Slavin, R.E., Madden, N.A., Dolan. L.l., Wasik, B.A., Ross, S. and Smith, L. (1994), *Success for All: Longitudunal Effects of Systematic School-by-School Reform in Seven Districts*. Paper presented to the annual meeting of the American Educational Research Association, New Orleans.

Smith, D. and Tomlinson, S. (1989), *The School Effect: A Study of Multiracial Comprehensives*. London: Policy Studies Institute.

SooHoo, S. (1993), 'Students as partners in research and restructuring schools', summer *Educational Forum*, 57, 386–93.

Southworth, G. (1994), 'The learning school' in P. Ribbens and E. Burridge (eds) *Improving Education: Promoting Quality in Schools*. London: Cassell.

St John-Brooks (1995), 'Universal quest for higher standards', *Times Educational Supplement*, 8, 9: 16.

Stallings, J. (1975), 'Implementation and child effects of teaching practices in follow through classrooms', *Monographs of the Society for Research in Child Development*, No. 163, 40, 7–8.

Stallings, J. and Hentzell, S. (1978), *Effective Teaching and Learning in Urban High Schools*, National Conference on Urban Education, Urban Education Program, CEMREL St Louis, MO.

Stebbins, L., St Pierre, R., Proper, E., Anderson, R. and Cerva, T. (1977), *Education as Experimentation: A Planned Variation Model, Vol IV: An Evaluation of Follow through*, Cambridge, MA: Abt Associates Inc.

Stedman, L. (1987), 'It's time we changed the effective schools formula', *Phi Delta Kappan*, 69, 3, 215–44.

Stenhouse, L. (1975), *An Introduction to Curriculum Research and Development*. London: Heinemann.

Stoll, L. and Fink, D. (1992), 'Effecting school change: the Halton approach', *School Effectiveness and School Improvement*, 3, 1, 19–41.

—   (1994), 'Views from the field: linking school effectiveness and school improvement', *School Effectiveness and School Improvement*, 5, 2, 149–77.

—   (1996), *Changing Our Schools: Linking School Effectiveness and School Improvement*. Buckingham: Open University Press.

Stoll, L. and Mortimore, P. (1995), *School Effectiveness and School Improvement*. Viewpoint No. 2. London: Institute of Education.

Stoll, L. and Thomson, M. (forthcoming), 'Moving together: a partnership approach to improvement' in P. Earley, B. Fidler and J. Ouston (eds) *Improvement through Inspection: Complementary Approaches to School Development*. London: David Fulton.

Stoll, L., Myers, K. and Reynolds, D. (1996), *Understanding Ineffectiveness*. Paper presented as part of the symposium 'International Advances in School Effectiveness Research and Practice', at the annual conference of the American Educational Research Association, New York, 9 April.

Stringfield, S. and Teddlie, C. (1987), 'A time to summarise: the Louisiana School Effectiveness Study', *Educational Leadership*, 46, 2: 48–9.

Stringfield, S., Teddlie, C. and Suarez, S. (1986), 'Classroom interaction in effective and ineffective schools: preliminary results from phase III of the Louisiana School Effectiveness Study', *Journal of Classroom Interaction*, 20, 2, 31–7.

Stringfield, S., Teddlie, C., Wimpleberg, R.K. and Kirby, P. (1992), 'A five year follow-up of schools in the Louisiana School Effectiveness Study' in J. Baslin and Z. Sass (eds) *School Effectiveness and Improvement Proceedings of the Third International Congress for School Effectiveness*. Jerusalem: Magness Press.

Tabberer, R. (1994), *School and Teacher Effectiveness*. Slough: NFER.

Teddlie, C. and Stringfield, S. (1993), *Schools Make a Difference: Lessons Learned from a 10 Year Study of School Effects*. New York: Teachers College Press.

Teddlie, C. and Virgilio, I. (1988), *School Context Differences across Grades: A Study of Teacher Behaviours*. Paper presented at the annual meeting of the American Educational Research Association, New Orleans.

Teddlie, C., Kirby, P. and Stringfield, S. (1989), 'Effective versus ineffective schools: observable differences in the classroom', *American Journal of Education*, 97, 3, 221–36.

TES (1996), *Inspectors to take account of deprivations*, February 23, 1.

Thomas, S. and Mortimore, P. (1994), 'Report on value added analysis of 1993 GCSE examination results in Lancashire' (in press), *Research Papers in Education*.

— (1996), 'Comparison of value-added models for secondary school effectiveness', *Research Papers in Education*, 11, 1, 5–33.

Thomas, S., Sammons, P. and Mortimore, P. (1994), *Stability and Consistency in Secondary Schools' Effects on Students' GCSE Outcomes*. Paper presented at the annual conference of the British Educational Research Association, 9 September, St Anne's College, University of Oxford.

— (1995), *Differential Secondary School Effectiveness*. Paper presented at the BERA annual conference, Bath 1995, *British Educational Research Journal* (forthcoming).

Tizard, B., Blatchford, P., Burke, J., Farquhar, C. and Plewis, I. (1988), *Young Children at School in the Inner City*. Hove: Lawrence Erlbaum Associates.

Tizard, J., Schofield, W. and Hewison, J. (1992), 'Symposium: reading-collaboration between teachers and parents in assisting children's reading', *British Journal of Educational Psychology*, 52, 1, 1–15.

Tooley, J. (1995), 'A measure of freedom', *TES*, July 7, 18.

Topping, K.J. (1992), 'Short- and long-term follow-up of parental involvement in reading projects', *British Educational Research Journal*, 18, 4, 369–79.

Trisman, D., Waller, M. and Wilder, C. (1976), *A Descriptive and Analytic Study of Compensatory Reading Programs*. Princetown: Educational Testing Service.

Tyler, R. (1949), *Basic Principles of Curriculum and Instruction*. Chicago and London: The University of Chicago Press.

Tymms, P. (1992), 'The relative effectiveness of post-16 institutions in England (including Assisted Places Scheme Schools)', *British Educational Research Journal*, 18, 2, 175–92.

United States Department of Education (1987), *What Works Research about Teaching and Learning*. Washington: United States Department of Education (revised edition).

United States General Accounting Office (1985), *Effective Schools Programs: Their Extent and Characteristics*. Washington DC: US General Accounting Office.

van der Grift, W (1987), 'Self-perceptions of educational leadership and average achievement', in J. Scheerens and W. Stoel (eds) *Effectiveness of School Organisations*. Lisse: Swets and Zeitlinger.

van Velzen, W., Miles, M., Ekholm. M., Hameyer, U. and Robin, D. (1985), *Making School Improvement Work: A Conceptual Guide to Practice*. Leuven, Belgium: Acco Publishers.

Venezky, R. and Winfield, L. (1979), *Schools that Succeed beyond Expectations in Teaching Reading*. Newark: University of Delaware.

Vulliamy, G. (1987), 'School effectiveness research in Tanzania', *Comparative Education*, 23, 2, 209–23.

Vygotsky, L.S. (1978), *Mind in Society*. Cambridge, Mass: MIT Press.

Walberg, H.J. (1984), 'Improving the productivity of American schools', *Educational Leadership*, 41, 19–27.

— (1985), 'Homework's powerful effects on learning', *Educational Leadership*, 42, 7, 76–9.

— (1986), 'Syntheses of research on teaching' in M.C. Wittrock (ed.), *Handbook of Research on Teaching*. New York: Macmillan.

Walsh, P. (1993), *Education and Meaning: Philosophy in Practice*. London: Cassell.

Wang, M.C., Haertel, G. and Walberg, J. (1993), 'Toward a knowledge base for school learning', *Review of Educational Research*, 63, 249–94.

Washington DC: Council for Basic Education.

Wayson, W. W. (1988), *Up from Excellence*. Phi Delta Kappa Inc.

Weber, G. (1971), *Inner-city Children Can Be Taught to Read: Four Successful Schools* (Occasional Paper 18) Washington D.C.: Council for Basic Education..

Weinberger, J. et al. (1990), *Ways of Working with Parents Early Literacy Development*. University of Sheffield.

Weindling, D. (1989), 'The process of school improvement: some practical messages from research', *School Organisation*, 9, 1.

West, M. and Hopkins, D. (1995), *Reconceptualising School Effectiveness and School Improvement*. Annual meeting of the British Educational Research Association and the European conference on Educational Research, Bath, 17 September.

White, J. (1990), *Education and the Good Life: Beyond the National Curriculum*. London: Kogan Page.

— (1996), *Philosophical Perspectives on School Effectiveness and School Improvement*. Paper presented at the annual conference of the British Educational Research Association, University of Lancaster.

Willms, J.D. (1992), *Monitoring School Performance: A Guide for Educators*. London: Falmer.

Willms, J.D. and Raudenbush, S.W. (1989), 'A longitudinal hierarchical linear model for estimating school effects and their stability', *Journal of Educational Measurement*, 26, 3, 209–32.

Wilson, B. and Corcoran, T. (1988), *Successful Secondary Schools*. London: Falmer Press.

Wilson, R. (1990), 'Sociology and the mathematical method' in A. Giddens and J. Turner (eds) *Social Theory Today*. London: Polity Press.

Wimpleberg et al. (1989), 'Sensitivity to context: the past and future of effective schools research', *Educational Administration Quarterly*, 25, 82–107.

Winch, C. (1996), *Quality and Education*. Oxford: Blackwell.

Witziers, B. (1994), *Coordination in Secondary Schools and its Implications for Student Achievement*. Paper presented at the annual conference of the American Educational Research Association, 4–8 April, New Orleans.

Wood, G.H. (1990), 'Teaching for democracy', *Educational Leadership*, 48, 3, November, 32–6.

Wood, R. and Power, C. (1987), 'Aspects of the competence-performance distinction: educational, psychological and measurement issues', *Journal of Curriculum Studies*, 19, 5, 409–24.

Woodhead, C. (1997) *Inspecting Schools: The Key to Raising Educational Standards*. 'The Last Word' lecture at the Royal Geographical Association, London, 21 January.

Woodhouse, G. and Goldstein, H. (1988), 'Educational performance indicators and LEA league tables', *Oxford Review of Education*, 14, 3.

Wringe, C. (1988), *Understanding Educational Aims*. London: Unwin Hyman.

Wynne, E. (1980), *Looking at Schools: Good, Bad and Indifferent*, Lexington: Heath.